LATINA CHRISTIANA

Introduction to Christian Latin

━ BOOK II ━

TEACHER MANUAL

Cheryl Lowe

CLASSICAL TRIVIUM CORE SERIES

LATINA CHRISTIANA II: TEACHER MANUAL

Third Edition © 2005 by Cheryl Lowe and Memoria Press
Original Copyright © 1998

ISBN 1-930953-06-2

www.memoriapress.com

Table of Contents

REVIEW LESSONS

The first five lessons review all of the vocabulary and forms from BOOK I. However, <u>new grammar material</u>, *the use of the accusative case for direct objects*, <u>is taught in Lessons 2-5,</u> so do not skip these lessons. This new grammar material was inserted into these review lessons so that students could learn a new skill using familiar words.

NOUNS

Declensions

There are five declensions in Latin, two of which were in **BOOK I.** The last three will be covered in this text in Lessons 18-24.

Cases

In **BOOK I** the nominative case was used for singular and plural subjects, singular and plural predicate nominatives, and adjectives. In **BOOK II,** Lesson 6, students will be given a chart which summarizes the functions of all of the cases. They will use the chart in *Drills A and B* of their Exercises.

(Chart from Lesson 6)

Singular

	Form	Meaning	Use
Nominative	mens-a	the (a) table	subject, predicate noun
Genitive	mens-ae	of the table	possessive, *of* phrases
Dative	mens-ae	to/for the table	indirect object
Accusative	mens-am	the (a) table	direct object
Ablative	mens-a	by/with/from the table	prepositional objects

Plural

	Form	Meaning	Use
Nominative	mens-ae	the tables	subject, predicate noun
Genitive	mens-arum	of the tables	possessive, *of* phrases
Dative	mens-is	to/for the tables	indirect object
Accusative	mens-as	the tables	direct object
Ablative	mens-is	by/with/from the tables	prepositional objects

In actual translation only two new cases will be used, the *accusative* and *ablative*. The accusative case is used for direct objects of verbs (Lessons 2-5) and the objects of some prepositions (Lesson 10). The ablative case is also used for prepositional objects (Lesson 10). Both of these skills will be practiced for the remainder of the book.

ADJECTIVES

Students will learn to make adjectives agree with their nouns in both the nominative and accusative cases and when the noun and its adjective are in different declensions (Lesson 20). Ten new adjectives are given in Lesson 25.

VERBS

There are four conjugations. Students learned the first two conjugations in three tenses in **BOOK I.** **BOOK II** will cover the last two conjugations in two tenses, the present and imperfect. Students will begin learning about the principal parts of verbs. Three tenses of the irregular linking verb *sum*, "to be", will be learned. New verbs are covered in Lessons 11-17.

Teaching Guidelines

In general, follow the teaching guidelines from Book I. *Three new sections in some lesson plans are:*

1. **Related Latin words/sayings:** Sayings or words students have had in previous lessons that contain a new vocabulary word.
2. **Nota bene:** Notes on mistakes students are likely to make, or confusions they are likely to experience.
3. **Ab extra:** Material of interest from our Christian and Classical heritage.

EXERCISES

The principal purpose of the exercises is for students to gain skills in recognizing and writing nouns, verbs and adjectives in their inflected forms.

The exercises in BOOK II are considerably more difficult than in BOOK I and students in grades 4-6 will need much help in doing them. Start by doing all of the exercises with your students in class and then gradually leave some of each exercise or drill to be done by the students alone as they gain confidence.

When students are translating sentences (Exercises A and B), especially beginning in Lesson VI, they will be using words from previous lessons. In order to prevent the frustration of continually looking up old words

1. Go over words (and any word facts needed) before students begin these two exercises.
2. Emphasize word mastery in your teaching so that students will rarely experience the need to look up a word in the index.

4th and 5th graders will need assistance in translating from English to Latin throughout the year.

EMPHASIZING MASTERY OF VOCABULARY AND FORMS

The failure to master vocabulary is the primary reason students become frustrated and want to quit Latin or any language study. Students who fail to retain vocabulary will find doing their exercises to be very time consuming and tedious. This should be prevented, if at all possible, by constant attention on the part of the teacher to Mastery learning. When something is mastered it becomes a part of the permanent memory and is there for the student to use when needed. There are two aids to memory which are imperative for even the best of students.

Call Cards

Students should have made vocabulary cards in the first year's study, but often good students may get by without them. As the words accumulate in the second year even students with the best of memories begin to confuse similar words and become frustrated at their forgetfulness. Memoria Press publishes *Latina Christiana* flash cards that are color coded according to part of speech. The set also includes all of the conjugations, declensions, cue words, and sayings and can be purchased from your favorite book supplier or online at *MemoriaPress.com*.

Alternatively, card stock in bright colors can be purchased at office supply stores and copy shops will cut card stock paper into 3x4 or 2x3 sizes for a minimal charge. Insist that all students make vocabulary cards and review them weekly. If this is practiced consistently students will be able to acquire a large vocabulary and to translate Latin with a minimum of frustration. **Suggested homework assignments** are given for a few of the first lessons to illustrate how you might want to use the CALL CARDS to correlate with each lesson.

Call Card Review Form

Students should be assigned a certain number of their vocabulary cards to review every week. A reproducible form is provided on page 5 for students to keep a permanent record of cards reviewed. (It may also be downloaded online at www.MemoriaPress.com on the Latina Christiana II page.) The *card group* could be *all nouns*, *all verbs*, *third declension nouns*, etc. Students should review words at least once each way, from Latin to English, and from English to Latin. Cards missed should be put in a left hand stack and reviewed again. The time required and the number of cards in the group can also be recorded. In drilling from English to Latin you may want to require students to write the Latin word in order to check their spelling.

During drill time at the beginning of every class, the teacher should <u>call out</u> the cards to students around the room. A student who misses a card may receive an appropriate punishment such as a *withering stare* or writing the word and its meaning 5 times on the board. CALL CARD time can be a fun time for most students. CALL CARD time informs the teacher about the level of vocabulary mastery among the students and which words are the most troublesome. Students will probably need to keep their CALL CARDS in a card file box, with dividers according to parts of speech and declension/conjugation.

Recitation

There is a strong tendency for Latin study to be visual because Latin is not a spoken language. However, hearing the forms, endings, principal parts, and vocabulary spoken aloud is a great aid to memory. Remind students to always say the words or forms they are learning at home <u>out loud.</u> In addition, <u>every class period should begin with oral recitation of all of forms and endings from Book I and those in Book II as they are added</u>, as well as prayers, songs, etc. After the oral recitation, do a CALL CARD drill.
This complete oral drill at the beginning of each class is essential.

SUGGESTED CLASS LESSON PLAN

1. Salutation. Recitation of prayers, memorized passages, all forms. Call Cards.
2. Review for quiz over previous week's vocabulary and forms.
3. Quiz
4. Check homework (exercises). Students should have papers ready and books open. Going around the room, students should <u>promptly</u> read question and give answer. Students should write sentence translations (Exercises A and B) on the board. A military-style discipline makes this time go quickly.
5. New Latin lesson. Work on exercises in class until students have confidence to do some alone.
6. History lesson.
7. Review time, games, songs.
8. Valete!

LATIN INSTRUCTIONAL DVDs

Last but not least, if you are looking for more help teaching Latin, Memoria Press publishes Latina Christiana Instructional DVDs. Leigh Lowe teaches each lesson thoroughly with helpful hints and tricks for learning Latin. The DVDs are a great resource for your students or as a model teaching guide for you.

Student Goals *for Second Year Latin*

A major goal for second year Latin is for students to practice writing and reading nouns, adjectives, and verbs in their <u>inflected forms</u>. The many exercises which require students to write and translate words in their inflected forms may seem tedious but they give students this needed practice in seeing and writing vocabulary words as they will appear in actual Latin sentences. To read Latin sentences, students must (1) identify the root of the word to know its meaning and (2) identify the inflected ending to know how the word is used in the sentence. It will take many years of practice before students can do this with speed and accuracy.

1. **Pronounce, spell and translate 200 Latin words from Book I, and 200 words from Book II.**

2. **Read and translate 25 Latin sayings from Book I and 20 sayings from Book II. Memorize additional prayers, passages, and songs from Book II.**

3. **Grammar**
   a. Define noun, verb, adjective and preposition.
   b. Understand concept of tense, person, and number.
   c. Conjugate 1st and 2nd conjugation verbs in present, imperfect, and future tenses, and 3rd and 4th conjugation verbs in the present and imperfect tenses.
   d. Give principal parts for regular and some irregular verbs of all four conjugations.
   e. Decline nouns in all five declensions.
   f. Use 1st/2nd declension adjectives in agreement with nouns in all declensions.
   g. Translate simple sentences with direct objects and prepositional phrases from English to Latin and Latin to English.

4. **Derivatives**
   a. Be exposed to many English words of Latin origin and use them correctly in sentences.

5. **History and Geography**
   a. Read stories 14-30 in Famous Men of Rome.
   b. Be familiar with three periods of Roman government, and decline of Roman civilization.
   c. Have some knowledge of Roman world at the time of the birth of Christ and the struggle between Christianity and paganism.

Call Cards Form *for vocabulary cards*

CALL CARDS FORM
(See Teaching Guidelines for Instructions)

Date	Card Group	# of Cards	L>E E>L	Cards in Left Stack	Time

Lesson Plans
& Keys

Lesson Plan I

The first five lessons are an excellent review of BOOK I.

WORD STUDY

All first and second conjugation verbs are listed from BOOK I. Now is the time to address problems such as difficult spellings, confusion about similar words: *habito* and *habeo*, *moneo* and *moveo, libero* and *laboro,* etc. There are 33 words in this review lesson. Students should master all forms, vocabulary, and sayings.

Vocabulary

1st Conjugation Verbs			2nd Conjugation Verbs	
amo	clamo	occupo	moneo	doceo
porto	voco	appello	video	debeo
laudo	supero	narro	terreo	prohibeo
oro	adoro	do	habeo	jubeo
laboro	libero	habito	moveo	sedeo
navigo	ambulo	lavo	timeo	
paro	pugno			
specto	judico			

Grammar Forms

Verb endings		1st Conjugation		2nd Conjugation	
S.	Pl.	S.	Pl.	S.	Pl.
Present tense					
o	mus	porto	portamus	moneo	monemus
s	tis	portas	portatis	mones	monetis
t	nt	portat	portant	monet	monent
Future tense					
bo	bimus	portabo	portabimus	monebo	monebimus
bis	bitis	portabis	portabitis	monebis	monebitis
bit	bunt	portabit	portabunt	monebit	monebunt
Imperfect tense					
bam	bamus	portabam	portabamus	monebam	monebamus
bas	batis	portabas	portabatis	monebas	monebatis
bat	bant	portabat	portabant	monebat	monebant

Present Tense Irregular Verbs

sum	sumus
es	estis
est	sunt
pos-sum	pos-sumus
pot-es	pot-estis
pot-est	pos-sunt

Latin Sayings

Ora et Labora
Mater Italiae - Roma
Caelum et Terra
E pluribus unum
Labor omnia vincit
mea culpa
Anno Domini, A.D.

Grammar

Summary of all work on conjugations and tenses. Students should know names of tenses, endings, and how to conjugate any verb in any tense, and its English meaning. A good way to study verbs for the next five review lessons is to play games (verb bee or gladiators) or do drills. Example: Give verb forms in either the English or Latin, e.g. *clamabamus* or *we were shouting,* and students compete to translate correctly.

New Grammar Lesson

There are three English translations for a Latin verb in the present tense.

Voco can mean   I call
                       I do call
                       I am calling

I do call is called the *emphatic* in English, and *I am calling* is called the *progressive.* There is no way to express the emphatic or progressive in Latin.

A. Give the three English translations for each verb.

1. portat ___he (she, it) carries, he does carry, he is carrying___
2. laudo ___I praise, I do praise, I am praising___
3. docetis ___you (pl.) teach, you do teach, you are teaching___
4. videmus ___we see, we do see, we are seeing___

B. Complete these sentences by adding "t" or "nt" to the verb. Translate three ways.

1. Puellae ora_nt_. The girls pray.
   The girls do pray.
   The girls are praying.

2. Servus ora_t_. The slave prays.
   The slave does pray.
   The slave is praying.

3. Nauta voca_t_. The sailor calls.
   The sailor does call.
   The sailor is calling.

4. Nautae voca_nt_. The sailors call.
   The sailors do call.
   The sailors are calling.

5. Servi sede_nt_. Slaves sit.
   Slaves do sit.
   Slaves are sitting.

6. Amicus sede_t_. The friend sits.
   The friend does sit.
   The friend is sitting.

7. Regnum supera_t_ The kingdom overcomes.
   The kingdom does overcome.
   The kingdom is overcoming.

8. Regna supera_nt_. Kingdoms overcome.
   Kingdoms do overcome.
   Kingdoms are overcoming.

C. Circle the tense ending and translate. [Teacher Aid]

1. lauda(bant) they were praising [3 pl imp]
2. ama(bimus) we will love [1 pl fut]
3. habita(batis) you (pl.) were living [2 pl imp]
4. mon(ent) they warn [3 pl pres]
5. doce(bat) he (she, it) was teaching [3 sg imp]
6. porta(bunt) they will carry [3 pl fut]
7. vide(bis) you will see [2 sg fut]
8. jube(bas) you were ordering (commanding) [2 sg imp]
9. judica(bam) I was judging, considering [1 sg imp]
10. habe(batis) you (pl.) were having [2 pl imp]

ASSIGNMENT

1) Assign **Call Cards** for all verbs in this lesson, L>E, E>L. Students should review with call cards until there are no cards in the left stack. Write frequently misspelled words, such as *appello, occupo*, several times. Students should know correct spelling of both Latin and English verbs.

2) Exercises.

3) Study for quiz over all words, forms and sayings.

Grammar Cont.

In English, *do, is, are, am* are helping verbs **and** verbs that can stand alone. This is confusing to students because there are no helping verbs in Latin, there are *helping endings* instead! Students will try to translate these helping verbs by adding the Latin forms for the verbs *be* and *do*. Remember *I am calling* is *voco*, not *sum voco*.

Present tense

voco	I call, I do call I am calling	**vocamus**	we call, we do call, we are calling
vocas	you call, you do call you are calling	**vocatis**	you call, you do call you are calling
vocat	he, she, it calls, does call, is calling	**vocant**	they call, they do call, they are calling

Lesson Plan I

PRONUNCIATION REVIEW

Alphabet
The Latin alphabet has no "w".
Words with "y" are of Greek origin.

Vowels
In Christian Latin vowels are usually long.

Vowel	Long	Example
a	'father' (ah)	ad, mater
e	'they' (ay)	me, video
i	'machine' (ee)	video, qui
o	'no' (oh)	porta, omnis
u	'rule' (oo)	cum, sumus

Sometimes the vowels e and i tend toward the short vowel sounds ('Ed','it') as in 'mensa' and 'et'.

Diphthongs and digraphs

Digraph	Pronunciation	Example
ae	like e in 'they' (ay)	saepe, praemium,
oe		proelium

Diphthong	Pronunciation	Example
au	like ou in out (ow)	laudo, nauta

Consonants
Most of the consonants are pronounced as in English, with the following exceptions.

Consonant	Pronunciation	Examples
c	before e, i, ae, oe, like ch in 'charity'	decem, cibus, caelum
c	before other letters, hard c as in 'cut'	clamo, culpa
g	soft before e, i, ae, oe as in 'gym'	regina, gemini
g	hard before other letters as in 'go'	gratia, fuga
gn	like gn as in 'lasagna'	pugno, regnum
j	like y as in 'yet'	judico, Jesus
s	like s as in 'sing' (never like z)	tres, mensa
sc	like sh	discipulus
t	when followed by i and a vowel, like tsee	gratia, tertius, nuntius

In words of three or more syllables, the accent mark indicates the stressed syllable. It is not necessary for the student to learn the location of the accent mark, or to copy it when writing Latin.

D. Translate. [see facing page for parsing teacher aid]

1. I am fighting. ___Pugno.___
2. They are preventing. ___Prohibent.___
3. She does wash. ___Lavat.___
4. They are not shouting. ___Non clamant.___
5. You (s.& pl.) do judge. ___Judicas (-atis).___
6. You (pl.) are giving. ___Datis.___
7. They do shout. ___Clamant.___
8. He is walking. ___Ambulat.___
9. They move. ___Movent.___
10. We do pray. ___Oramus.___

E. Conjugate in the present, imperfect and future.

1.
do	damus
das	datis
dat	dant

dabam	dabamus
dabas	dabatis
dabat	dabant

dabo	dabimus
dabis	dabitis
dabit	dabunt

2.
jubeo	jubemus
jubes	jubetis
jubet	jubent

jubebam	jubebamus
jubebas	jubebatis
jubebat	jubebant

jubebo	jubebimus
jubebis	jubebitus
jubebit	jubebunt

F. Use each derivative in a sentence.

1. amateur _____
2. vocal _____
3. laudable _____
4. ambulance _____
5. laboratory _____
6. narrator _____
7. spectator _____
8. timid _____

UPDATES

We have updated some exercises in this Third Edition Teacher Manual that **may** differ from your student book. The original exercises are listed below, but you should have the students use the updated exercises you will find on the lesson pages in this teacher manual. We have marked changed exercises with **.

The original exercises are not necessarily wrong. In most cases, they have been edited because they conflict with a Latin rule that is beyond the scope of this text.

Lesson Exercise #	**Original Question** **Original Answer**
III Exercise A #4	Christus discipulos docet. Christ teaches disciples.
VIII Exercise B #2	The teacher was teaching the students. Magister discipulos docebat.
XIII Exercise B #3	A man will answer the letter. Vir epistulam respondebit.
XVIII Drill B #1	with good will cum voluntate
XIX Exercise B #5	The sun was moving across the heavens Sol trans caelos movebat (caelum is neuter in the singular and masculine in the plural)
XXI Exercise A #5	Multi oves et agni in rure sunt. Many sheep and lambs are in the countryside.
XXI Exercise B #3	The soldiers are fighting in the river. Milites in rure pugnant
XXII Exercise B #4	The guards open the gates for a long time Custodes portas diu aperiunt
XXV Exercise B #4	The Romans were fighting with foreign tribes. Romani cum gentibus alienis pugnabant.

Lesson Plan II

WORD STUDY

Students should know all vocabulary, forms, and sayings. There are 46 first declension nouns in addition to the declension of the personal pronouns. Stress that the genitive singular ending for 1st declension nouns is *ae*.

Vocabulary

Roma, ae	mensa	
Italia, ae	toga	
gloria	patria	
vita	culpa	
aqua	Maria	
memoria	fuga	
victoria	luna	

terra	unda
lingua	Hispania
via	silva
fortuna	stella
herba	ursa
nauta	ira
Gallia	gratia
femina	hora
filia	pecunia

regina	ecclesia
puella	aquila
corona	aurora
mora	auriga
insula	pugna
injuria	fenestra
cena	fama

Grammar Forms
Case Endings

	S.	Pl.
nominative	a	ae
genitive	ae	arum
dative	ae	is
accusative	am	as
ablative	a	is

Noun Forms

	S.	Pl.
nominative	mens-a	mens-ae
genitive	mens-ae	mens-arum
dative	mens-ae	mens-is
accusative	mens-am	mens-as
ablative	mens-a	mens-is

Pronoun Forms
First person

S.	Pl.
ego	nos
mei	nostri, nostrum
mihi	nobis
me	nos
me	nobis

Second person

S.	Pl.
tu	vos
tui	vestri, vestrum
tibi	vobis
te	vos
te	vobis

Latin Sayings

Semper Fidelis

Senatus Populusque Romanus, S.P.Q.R.

stupor mundi

ante bellum

Excelsior

Sanctus, Sanctus, Sanctus, Dominus Deus Sabaoth

Grammar

Review declensions, formation of plurals in the nominative case, and names of cases.

New Grammar Lesson

Today we will learn how to make sentences with action verbs and direct objects. An action verb describes an action, whether mental, like *love*, or physical, like *fight*. "The slave calls" is a sentence with an action verb, but no direct object. But what if we say:

The slave calls Mary.

Rules

- The subject is the person or thing that performs the action of the verb.
- The direct object is the person or thing that receives the action of the verb.

Grammar

1. List all five Latin cases.
   nominative
   genitive
   dative
   accusative
   ablative

2. A word that receives the action of a verb is a __direct object__.

3. The direct object is always in the __accusative__ case.

4. Fill in these boxes with the normal word order of a Latin sentence.

subject	direct object	verb

Drill A. Write these nouns in the accusative singular and plural.

1. cena __cenam__   3. herba __herbam__
        __cenas__   __herbas__
2. hora __horam__   4. toga __togam__
        __horas__   __togas__

Drill B. Identify the case and number of these noun forms. For some words there will be more than one answer.

1. viam   accusative singular   [All 1st declension]
2. pecuniae   genitive, dative singular; nominative plural
3. memoriis   dative, ablative plural
4. fugarum   genitive plural
5. culpa   nominative, ablative singular

ASSIGNMENT

1) Drill with **CALL CARDS** for vocabulary in this lesson.

2) Exercises.

3) Learn definitions of subject and direct object.

4) Study for quiz over all forms, sayings and vocabulary.

Grammar Cont.

The *subject* is *slave*, the *action verb* is *calls,* but what function does the noun *Mary* have in this sentence? It is the *direct object* that receives the action of the verb. (You might illustrate a direct object by saying *I hit the table* while hitting the table.) The table receives the action of the verb.

We know how to say *slave* and *calls*, but how do we say *Mary*? *The direct object is written in the accusative case.* Write all of the case endings for the first declension on the board and have a student circle the accusative endings, *am* and *as*. In Latin the verb usually stands last in the sentence so the sentence would look like this.

Servus Mariam vocat.
The slave calls Mary

The model for this type of sentence is: **subject**   **direct object**   **action verb**
                                            sub.   *d.o.*   *a.v.*

Lesson Plan II

Exercise A. Underline the direct object and translate.

Translate verbs three ways. (except # 4)

1. Puella <u>cenam</u> parat. _____ The girl is preparing dinner. _____
   _____ prepares _____ does prepare _____ is preparing

2. Roma <u>insulas</u> occupat. _____ Rome is seizing the islands. _____
   _____ seizes _____ does seize _____ is seizing

3. Maria <u>fenestras</u> lavat. _____ Mary is washing the windows. _____
   _____ washes _____ does wash _____ is washing

4. Femina <u>aquam</u> portabit. _____ A woman will carry water. _____

5. Filia <u>stellas</u> videt. _____ The daughter sees the stars. _____
   _____ sees _____ does see _____ is seeing

Exercise B. Underline direct object and translate into Latin.

1. We are preparing <u>dinner</u>. _____ Cenam paramus. _____
2. The girls are moving <u>the tables</u>. _____ Puellae mensas movent. _____
3. The Queen has <u>a crown</u>. _____ Regina coronam habet. _____
4. The waves frighten <u>the girls</u>. _____ Undae puellas terrent. _____

Derivatives. Use each derivative in a sentence.

1. lunar _____
2. stellar _____
3. peninsula _____
4. glorious _____
5. coronation _____

Grammar

Translate these sentences:

Femina fenestram lavat.
The woman washes
the window.

Femina fenestras lavat.
The woman washes
the windows.

Nauta lunam videt.
The sailor sees
the moon.

Regina gloriam amat.
The queen loves
glory.

Lesson Plan II

Lesson Plan III

WORD STUDY

Second declension nouns, both masculine and neuter, 47 words in all. Learn all forms, sayings, and vocabulary. Emphasize that the genitive singular ending for 2nd declension nouns is always *i*.

The nominative singular can end in *us* and *um*. Because the nominative endings of nouns can vary, the **genitive** is <u>always </u>used to (a) identify the declension and (b) find the stem.
This is true for all five declensions.

Vocabulary

Masculine	Neuter
servus, i	bellum, i
amicus, i	donum, i
annus	oppidum
filius	telum
dominus	verbum
Deus	regnum
Christus	frumentum
legatus	signum
discipulus	imperium
gladius	proelium
murus	gaudium
populus	auxilium
animus	debitum
mundus	caelum
socius	peccatum
nuntius	vallum
barbarus	praemium
campus	vinum
capillus	tergum
cibus	forum
equus	
ventus	
locus	
agnus	
oculus	
hortus	
nimbus	
ludus	

Grammar Forms

Masculine

Case endings

S.	Pl.
us	i
i	orum
o	is
um	os
o	is

Noun Forms

serv-us	serv-i
serv-i	serv-orum
serv-o	serv-is
serv-um	serv-os
serv-o	serv-is

Neuter

Case Endings

um	a
i	orum
o	is
um	a
o	is

Noun Forms

don-um	don-a
don-i	don-orum
don-o	don-is
don-um	don-a
don-o	don-is

Latin Sayings

Novus ordo seclorum
Nunc aut numquam
Veni, vidi, vici
Agnus Dei, qui tollis peccata mundi.
Rident stolidi verba Latina
Quo vadis

Grammar

Review the plural forms of these nouns in the nominative case.

New Grammar Lesson

Teach the accusative of the second declension masculine. (The neuter accusative will be taught in lesson 4.) Write the masculine case endings on the board and have a student circle the nominative and accusative endings. Once students have identified the endings, they should be ready to translate sentences with direct objects in the second declension masculine.

English word order:	**The slave calls the friend.** *sub.* *a.v.* *d.o.*
Usual Latin word order:	**Servus amicum vocat.** *sub.* *d.o.* *a.v.*

Grammar

Grammar

1. A word that *receives* the action of a verb is a <u>direct object</u> and is put in the <u>accusative</u> case.

2. The person or thing that *performs* the action of the verb is the <u>subject</u> and is put in the <u>nominative</u> case.

3. The genitive singular of first declension nouns is <u>ae</u> and of second declension nouns is <u>i</u>.

ASSIGNMENT
1) **CALL CARDS**

2) Exercises

3) Study for quiz

Drill A. Give the accusative singular and plural of these second declension masculine nouns.

1. capillus	capillum	capillos
2. oculus	oculum	oculos
3. nimbus	nimbum	nimbos
4. campus	campum	campos

Drill B. Identify the case and number of these noun forms. For some words there will be more than one answer.

1. vento — dative, ablative singular   [All 2nd declension]
2. sociis — dative, ablative plural
3. amicorum — genitive plural
4. equi — genitive singular; nominative plural
5. agnum — accusative singular

Grammar Cont.

Classroom Exercises

Singular subjects and direct objects.

The barbarian carries a sword.   **Barbarus gladium portat.**
The woman prepares food.   **Femina cibum parat.**

Plural direct objects.

The barbarian carries swords.   **Barbarus gladios portat.**
The woman prepares foods.   **Femina cibos parat.**

Plural subjects and direct objects.

Barbarians carry swords.   **Barbari gladios portant.**
The women prepare foods.   **Feminae cibos parant.**

Lesson Plan III

Exercise A. Underline the direct object and translate.
For 1 & 2 translate verbs three ways.

1. Deus <u>mundum</u> amat.　　　　　God loves the world.
　　　　　　　　　　　　　　　　loves　　　does love　is loving
2. Roma <u>barbaros</u> superat.　　　Roma conquers the barbarians.
　　　　　　　　　　　　　　　　conquers　does conquer　is conquering
3. Legatus <u>gladium</u> portat.　　　The lieutenant carries a sword.
4. Christus <u>discipulos</u> habet.　　Christ has disciples.
5. Amicus <u>hortum</u> spectabat.　　The friend was looking at the garden.

Exercise B. Underline direct object and translate into Latin.

1. The town has <u>an ally</u>.　　　　Oppidum socium habet.
2. The master frees <u>the slaves</u>.　Dominus servos liberat.
3. The lieutenant sees <u>the horses</u>.　Legatus equos videt.
4. The people fear <u>the Lord</u>.　　Populus Dominum timet.
5. The son sees <u>the winds</u> and <u>the clouds</u>.　Filius ventos et nimbos videt.

Derivatives. Use each derivative in a sentence.

1. social _____
2. donate _____
3. discipline _____
4. annual _____
5. mural _____

~ 18 ~

Lesson Plan IV

WORD STUDY

These third declension nouns need much practice. Teach all vocabulary and sayings for mastery. Focus on the vowel changes between the nominative and the genitive. The genitive singular ending for 3rd declension nouns is *is*.

The italicized letters after some nouns indicate gender: masculine, feminine, common (either), and neuter. Ignore them for now.

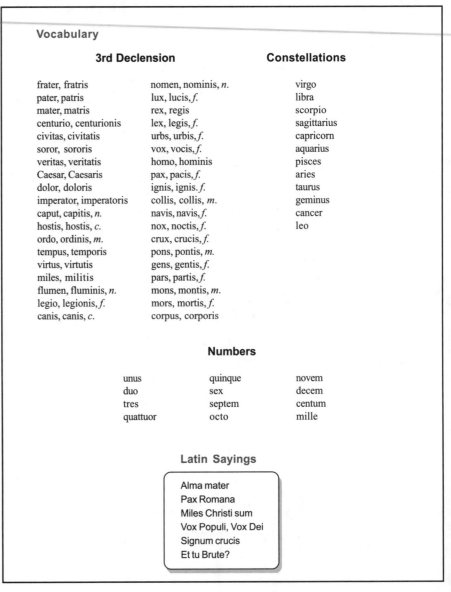

Vocabulary

3rd Declension		Constellations
frater, fratris	nomen, nominis, *n.*	virgo
pater, patris	lux, lucis, *f.*	libra
mater, matris	rex, regis	scorpio
centurio, centurionis	lex, legis, *f.*	sagittarius
civitas, civitatis	urbs, urbis, *f.*	capricorn
soror, sororis	vox, vocis, *f.*	aquarius
veritas, veritatis	homo, hominis	pisces
Caesar, Caesaris	pax, pacis, *f.*	aries
dolor, doloris	ignis, ignis. *f.*	taurus
imperator, imperatoris	collis, collis, *m.*	geminus
caput, capitis, *n.*	navis, navis, *f.*	cancer
hostis, hostis, *c.*	nox, noctis, *f.*	leo
ordo, ordinis, *m.*	crux, crucis, *f.*	
tempus, temporis	pons, pontis, *m.*	
virtus, virtutis	gens, gentis, *f.*	
miles, militis	pars, partis, *f.*	
flumen, fluminis, *n.*	mons, montis, *m.*	
legio, legionis, *f.*	mors, mortis, *f.*	
canis, canis, *c.*	corpus, corporis	

Numbers

unus	quinque	novem
duo	sex	decem
tres	septem	centum
quattuor	octo	mille

Latin Sayings

Alma mater
Pax Romana
Miles Christi sum
Vox Populi, Vox Dei
Signum crucis
Et tu Brute?

Grammar

Students will learn the declension of these nouns later this year. For this lesson continue teaching students how to write direct objects in the accusative case, this time in the 2nd declension neuter. Write the 2nd declension neuter endings on the board and circle the nominative and accusative endings. *It is a characteristic of all neuter nouns in Latin that the nominative and accusative case endings are the same, in both the singular and plural.* Practice writing and translating sentences on the board. Students will confuse the nominative singular of first declension nouns with the nominative and accusative plural of second declension neuter nouns. In the sentences to the right, *Roma* is a singular subject, but *dona* is a plural direct object.

Grammar. Give the nominative and genitive *singular* endings for each declension.

1.

	First Declension	Second Declension	Third Declension
nominative	a	us, um	varies
genitive	ae	i	is

2. What case is used to (a) identify the declension? ___genitive___

  (b) find the stem? ___genitive___ Why? __the genitive is the same__

  ___for all words in a declension, but the nominative can vary___

Drill A. Give the genitive singular for each Third Declension noun. Translate.

1. dolor ___doloris___ ___pain, sorrow___
2. mors ___mortis___ ___death___
3. civitas ___civitatis___ ___state___
4. miles ___militis___ ___soldier___
5. homo ___hominis___ ___man___
6. caput ___capitis___ ___head___
7. nomen ___nominis___ ___name___
8. flumen ___fluminis___ ___river___
9. nox ___noctis___ ___night___

Drill B. Give the acc. sing. and pl. of these 2nd decl. neuter nouns from Lesson III.

1. tergum ___tergum___ ___terga___ 3. auxilium ___auxilium___ ___auxilia___
2. proelium ___proelium___ ___proelia___ 4. praemium ___praemium___ ___praemia___

Grammar Cont.

Roma vallum habet.	Rome has a wall.
Deus dona dat.	God gives gifts.
Miles signa spectat.	The soldier looks at the signs.
Mater bellum timet.	Mother fears war.
Imperator oppidum terret.	The general frightens the town.

Lesson Plan IV

Drill C. Give the case and number of these noun forms.
For some there will be more than one answer. Nouns are from Lesson III.

		Case	Number	
1.	gaudio	dat., abl.	singular	[2nd decl n.]
2.	fora	nom., acc.	plural	[1st decl. f.]
3.	debitorum	gen.	plural	[2nd decl. n.]
4.	belli	gen.	singular	[2nd decl. n.]
5.	caelis	dat., abl.	plural	[2nd decl.*]

* caelum is neuter in the singular but masculine in the plural

Exercise A. Underline the direct object and translate.

1. Miles <u>tela</u> parabat.   The soldier was preparing weapons.
2. Dominus <u>praemia</u> dat.   The Lord gives rewards.
3. Roma <u>oppida</u> occupat.   Rome is seizing the towns.
4. Navis <u>frumentum</u> portat.   The ship is carrying grain.

Exercise B. Translate into Latin.

1. Mother does not like wars. (Use the verb *amo* for like)   Mater bella non amat.
2. Caesar likes battles.   Caesar proelia amat.
3. The city has a rampart.   Urbs vallum habet.
4. The emperor is giving a gift.   Imperator donum dat.

Derivatives. Use each derivative in a sentence.

1. virtue _____
2. regal _____
3. legislature _____
4. nocturnal _____
5. patriarch _____

Lesson Plan V

WORD STUDY

Students confuse *totus, tutus,* and *tuus*, as well as *magnus, malus* and *multus*. Review the definition of adjective.

Adjectives

altus, a, um
bonus, a, um
longus
malus
multus
magnus
plenus
sanctus
tutus
parvus
aeternus
certus
primus
secundus
tertius
proximus
summus
totus
solus
novus
tuus
meus

Adverbs

semper
saepe
nunc
clam
non
bene
numquam

Prepositions

ante
post
inter
contra
sub
supra
ex

Other Words

Jesus
sicut
et

Grammar Forms

First and Second Declension Adjectives

Masc.	Fem.	Neut.
Singular		
bon-us	bon-a	bon-um
bon-i	bon-ae	bon-i
bon-o	bon-ae	bon-o
bon-um	bon-am	bon-um
bon-o	bon-a	bon-o
Plural		
bon-i	bon-ae	bon-a
bon-orum	bon-arum	bon-orum
bon-is	bon-is	bon-is
bon-os	bon-as	bon-a
bon-is	bon-is	bon-is

Grammar

From Book I, review the lesson on adjectives, gender and agreement between adjectives and their nouns in *gender*, *number* and *case*. Last year we learned that in Latin adjectives can be written either before or after the noun. *The general rule is that adjectives of quantity (size, how many) precede their nouns and adjectives of quality (good, new, etc.) follow their nouns.*

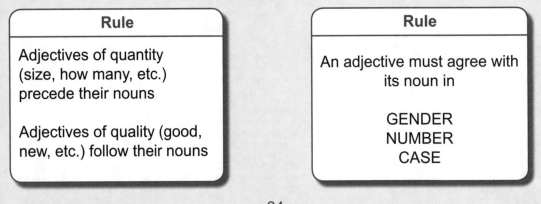

Rule

Adjectives of quantity (size, how many, etc.) precede their nouns

Adjectives of quality (good, new, etc.) follow their nouns

Rule

An adjective must agree with its noun in

GENDER
NUMBER
CASE

Grammar

1. Define *adjective*. <u>An adjective is a word that modifies a noun or a pronoun</u>.
2. Adjectives agree with their nouns in <u>gender</u>, <u>number</u>, and <u>case</u>.
3. The three genders of nouns in Latin are <u>masculine</u>, <u>feminine</u>, and <u>neuter</u>.

Exercise A. Underline the direct object and its adjective. Translate.

1. Regina <u>parvum filium</u> amat. <u>The queen loves the small son.</u>

2. Frater <u>multum cibum</u> habet. <u>Brother has much food.</u>

3. Barbari <u>multos capillos</u> habent. <u>The barbarians have many hairs (much hair).</u>

4. Rex <u>proxima oppida</u> occupabat. <u>The king was seizing the nearest towns.</u>

5. Puellae <u>filium meum</u> laudabunt. <u>The girls will praise my son.</u>

Exercise B. Underline the subject and its adjective. Translate.

1. <u>Filius meus</u> filiam tuam amat. <u>My son loves your daughter.</u>

2. <u>Servus malus</u> equos terrebat. <u>The bad slave was frightening the horses.</u>

3. <u>Legatus novus</u> puellas vocabit. <u>The new lieutenant will call the girls.</u>

4. <u>Magnae feminae</u> longas mensas movent. <u>The large women are moving the long tables.</u>

5. <u>Sanctus Deus</u> peccata non amat. <u>A Holy God does not like sins.</u>

Grammar Cont.

New Grammar Lesson

Now that we are using the accusative case, students must think about the case of the noun before they write its adjective.

Mary calls the *good girl*.	Maria *puellam bonam* vocat.
Good Mary calls the girl.	*Maria bona* puellam vocat.
The Queen calls the *small woman*.	Regina *parvam feminam* vocat.
The *small Queen* calls the woman.	*Parva regina* feminam vocat.

Lesson Plan V

Exercise C. Translate into Latin.

1. Your daughter adores horses.   Filia tua equos adorat.

2. He will see the high wall.   Altum vallum videbit.

3. Rome loves great glory.   Roma magnam gloriam amat.

4. God gives eternal life.   Deus vitam aeternam dat.

Derivatives. Use a derivative from today's lesson.

1. A large number of people or things is a   multitude   .
2. An answer that is close but not exact is   approximate   .
3.   Sanctify   means to make holy.
4. Gorillas like   plenty   of bananas.

Lesson Plan V

Review Lesson A

Drill A. Mark the correct case or cases and number. Translate.

		Nom.	Acc.	S.	Pl.	Meaning	
1.	loci	X			X	places	[2nd decl.]
2.	gaudium	X	X	X		joy	[2nd decl.]
3.	barbarum		X	X		barbarian	[2nd decl.]
4.	peccata	X	X		X	sins	[2nd decl.]
5.	fama	X		X		fame	[1st decl.]
6.	tergum	X	X	X		back	[2nd decl.]
7.	muros		X		X	walls	[2nd decl.]
8.	hortum		X	X		garden	[2nd decl.]
9.	debita	X	X		X	debts	[2nd decl.]
10.	fuga	X		X		flight	[1st decl.]
11.	morae	X			X	delays	[1st decl.]
12.	auxilium	X	X	X		help	[2nd decl.]

READING # 1
Jesus Christus

Jesus est homo. Jesus est Deus. Jesus et homo et[1] Deus est. Jesus puellas et feminas et pueros et homines[2] amat. Jesus servos et nautas et discipulos amat. Jesus in[3] mundum venit[4]. Jesus in terra ambulabat. Jesus multas fabulas narrabat. Jesus in aqua ambulabat. Jesus mundum superabat. Jesus nunc est in Caelo[5]. Jesus est Christus.

---

[1] et...et, both... and
[2] acc. pl. of homo
[3] into (in subsequent sentences in means *in* or *on*)
[4] came
[5] Heaven

Assignment

Assign students full set of **CALL CARDS** for **BOOK I**. Vocabulary and forms for first year should be mastered thoroughly, before the 200 new words in this book are begun. At this point students will still be making many mistakes in using the accusative case and in translating and this is not a problem. Failure to master the vocabulary is a problem. The grammar and sentence translation sections of the Exercises should also be studied for the test.

Reading #1

Jesus is a man. Jesus is God. Jesus is both man and God. Jesus loves girls and women, boys and men. Jesus loves slaves, sailors and students. Jesus came into the world. Jesus was walking on the earth. Jesus was telling many stories. Jesus was walking on water. Jesus was overcoming the world. Jesus now is in Heaven. Jesus is the Christ.

The imperfect tense is the only past tense student know and will be used in this book even though it often sounds awkward. The Latin imperfect can sometimes be translated by the English past tense, depending on the context, and may be so translated this year for convenience in these readings. (Jesus walked on the earth, told many stories, walked on water, etc.)

Lesson Plan VI

SAYING

This is an abbreviated form of *Vade retro me Satana,* in Mark 8:33, where Jesus rebukes Peter for having in mind the things of the world instead of God.

A similar saying is *Apage Satanas*, *Away with thee, Satan*, in Matt. 4:10, where Jesus rebukes Satan during his temptation in the wilderness. These are useful expressions for us today since we still struggle with temptation.

ASSIGNMENT

(1) Tape exercise form for Lesson VI

(2) Exercises

(3) Study for quiz over vocabulary and saying

(4) **CALL CARDS** for all first declension nouns (Lessons II and VI), L>E, E>L. Begin learning some of the conversational Latin and some of the selections for memorization.

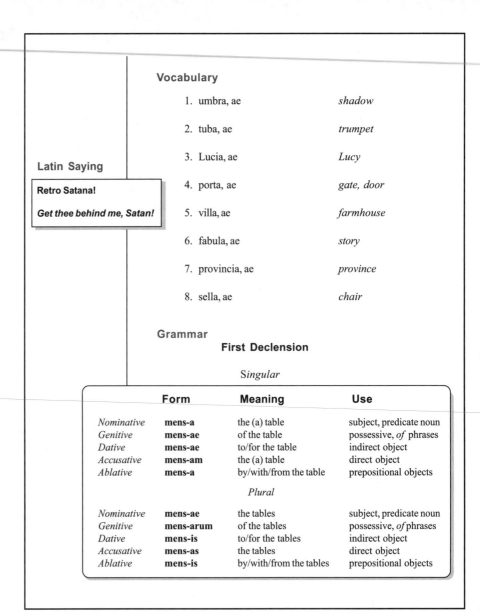

Latin Saying

Retro Satana!

Get thee behind me, Satan!

Vocabulary

1.	umbra, ae	*shadow*
2.	tuba, ae	*trumpet*
3.	Lucia, ae	*Lucy*
4.	porta, ae	*gate, door*
5.	villa, ae	*farmhouse*
6.	fabula, ae	*story*
7.	provincia, ae	*province*
8.	sella, ae	*chair*

Grammar

First Declension

Singular

	Form	Meaning	Use
Nominative	mens-a	the (a) table	subject, predicate noun
Genitive	mens-ae	of the table	possessive, *of* phrases
Dative	mens-ae	to/for the table	indirect object
Accusative	mens-am	the (a) table	direct object
Ablative	mens-a	by/with/from the table	prepositional objects

Plural

Nominative	mens-ae	the tables	subject, predicate noun
Genitive	mens-arum	of the tables	possessive, *of* phrases
Dative	mens-is	to/for the tables	indirect object
Accusative	mens-as	the tables	direct object
Ablative	mens-is	by/with/from the tables	prepositional objects

Grammar

This chart is traditional in Latin books and gives students the approximate meanings of the cases they have learned.

The <u>genitive</u> case is used to express possession and most *of phrases* in English. The <u>dative</u> case is used for indirect objects and many *to/for phrases* in English. These two cases will not be used in sentences this year, but will be used in the drills.

The accusative and ablative cases are used for objects of prepositions which will be taught in Lesson 10.

The ablative case is often used without prepositions to mean *by, with,* or *from.* The ablative case is called the *by/with/from* case.

Lesson Plan VI

Grammar

1. The ablative case is the ___by, with, from___ case.
2. The dative case is the ___to, for___ case.

Drill A. Identify case and number. Translate using meanings from table.
Some words will have more than one answer.   [All 1st declension]

1. umbrarum gen.   plural   of the shadows
2. villam   acc.   singular   the (a) farmhouse
3. sellas   acc.   plural   chairs
4. portis   dat., abl.   plural   to, for the gates; by, with, from the gates
5. fabulas   acc.   plural   the stories
6. Lucia   nom., abl.   singular   Lucy; by, with, from Lucy
7. provinciae gen., dat. sing.; nom. pl. of the province; to, for the province; the provinces
8. tubis   dat., abl.   plural   to, for the trumpets; by, with, from the trumpets
9. umbras   acc.   plural   shadows

Drill B. Verb review. Translate.

1. We will fear. ___Timebimus.___ [1 pl fut; 2nd conj.]
2. They were commanding. ___Jubebant.___ [3 pl imp; 2nd conj.]
3. You (s.) do work. ___Laboras.___ [2 sg pres; 1st conj.]
4. You (pl.) owe. ___Debetis.___ [2 pl pres; 2nd conj.]
5. I will overcome. ___Superabo.___ [1 sg fut; 1st conj.]
6. He is adoring. ___Adorat.___ [3 sg pres; 1st conj.]
7. We were fighting. ___Pugnabamus.___ [1 pl imp; 1st conj.]
8. They will live. ___Habitabunt.___ [3 pl fut; 1st conj.]

DERIVATIVES

umbra, ae	*umbrella*
tuba, ae	*tube*
porta, ae	*porch*
	portal
	porthole
villa, ae	*village*
	villain
fabula, ae	*fable*
	fabulous

Grammar Cont.

In lessons 6-9, Drill A exercises will give the nouns from that lesson in the various case forms. These exercises help students to recognize nouns in their inflected forms.

Over the next several lessons students should become very familiar with this chart and eventually commit it to memory.

Lesson Plan VI

Exercise A.   Translate sentences with <u>adjectives modifying subjects.</u>

1. <u>Lucia bona</u> fabulas narrabit.   <u>Good Lucy will tell stories.</u>
2. <u>Memoriae bonae</u> gaudium dant.   <u>Good memories give joy.</u>
3. <u>Amicus meus</u> aquilam videt.   <u>My friend sees an eagle.</u>
4. <u>Parva puella</u> equum vocabat.   <u>A small girl was calling the horse.</u>
5. <u>Miles malus</u> villam occupat.   <u>A bad soldier seizes the farmhouse.</u>

Exercise B.   Translate into Latin.   Remember the usual word order of a Latin sentence.

1. Lucy was moving the chairs.   <u>Lucia sellas movebat.</u>
2. Rome was seizing the province.   <u>Roma provinciam occupabat.</u>
3. The girls will carry the trumpets.   <u>Puellae tubas portabunt.</u>
4. Lucy sees the shadow.   <u>Lucia umbram videt.</u>
5. The farmhouse has new gates.   <u>Villa portas novas habet.</u>

Derivatives.   Use each derivative in a sentence.

1. fabulous _____
2. umbrella _____
3. portal _____
4. province _____

Lesson Plan VII

SAYING

This aphorism suggests the slow continuous processes by which all *natural* events occur. Evolutionists, recognizing the truth of this expression, conceived of the evolutionary process as one of slow continuous change with innumerable intermediate forms. The crises in contemporary evolutionary theory stems from these leaps (gaps) between organisms; the near total absence of intermediate forms. Nature does not make leaps -- but God may! Modern taxonomy was founded in 1735 by Carl Linnaeus with his *Systema Naturae*, written in Latin, of course, and based on a study of the profound discontinuity (gaps) between living organisms and their inability to cross natural boundaries.

Latin Saying

Natura non facit saltum

Nature does not make leaps

Vocabulary

1.	scientia, ae	*knowledge*
2.	ara, ae	*altar*
3.	casa, ae	*cottage*
4.	cithara, ae	*harp*
5.	taberna, ae	*shop*
6.	natura, ae	*nature*
7.	janua, ae	*door, entrance*
8.	epistula, ae	*letter*
9.	tabella, ae	*tablet*
10.	culina, ae	*kitchen*
11.	agricola, ae, *m.*	*farmer*
12.	poeta, ae, *m.*	*poet*

Grammar

There are no new forms this week. Use time to drill on any forms and vocabulary in which students are weak. Continue to teach the chart in Lesson VI.

Grammar

1. The stem of a Latin noun is always found by dropping the ending from the
   <u>genitive singular</u>.

2. All nouns whose genitive singular ends in **ae** belong to the <u>first</u>
   declension.

3. Three first-declension nouns that are masculine are <u>nauta</u>, <u>poeta</u>,
   and <u>agricola</u>.

Drill A. Identify case and number. Translate using meanings from table.
Some words will have more than one answer.   [All 1st declension]

1. tabernae — gen., dat. sing.; nom. pl. — of the shop; to, for the shop
2. epistularum — gen. pl. — of the letters
3. januas — acc. pl. — doors
4. citharis — dat., abl. pl. — to, for the harps; by, with, from the harps
5. culinarum — gen. pl. — of the kitchens
6. poetis — dat., abl. pl. — to, for the poets; by with, from the poets
7. ara — nom, abl. sing, — altar; by, with, from the altar
8. scientiam — acc. sing. — knowledge

Drill B. Decline.

1.

janua nova	januae novae
januae novae	januarum novarum
januae novae	januis novis
januam novam	januas novas
janua nova	januis novis

2.

poeta bonus	poetae boni
poetae boni	poetarum bonorum
poetae bono	poetis bonis
poetam bonum	poetas bonos
poeta bono	poetis bonis

WORD STUDY

A *tabella* is a small tablet like a student would carry. A *villa* from lesson VI was a large country estate of a wealthy person. A *casa* would be a small country house of a peasant. *Agricola, nauta* and *poeta* are rare exceptions to the rule that all first decl. nouns are feminine. These words are masculine because only men were farmers, sailors, and poets. They are declined just like other first decl. nouns. (When writing an adjective modifying these words the adjective must be written in the masculine form.)

DERIVATIVES

scientia, ae	*science*
	conscience
	conscious
	omniscient
casa	*casino*
cithara, ae	*guitar*
taberna, ae	*tavern*
	tabernacle
natura, ae	*natural*
janua, ae	*Janus*
	janitor
	January
epistula, ae	*epistle*
culina, ae	*culinary*
	kiln
agricola, ae	*agriculture*
poeta, ae	*poetry*

Lesson Plan VII

Exercise A. Translate these sentences with <u>adjectives modifying direct objects</u>.

1. Roma <u>multas terras</u> superabit. ___Rome will overcome many lands.___

_____

2. Imperator <u>multa oppida</u> superabat. _____

___The general was conquering many towns.___

3. Populus <u>longa bella</u> non amat. ___The people do not like long wars.___

___['populus' is singular in Latin athough 'people' is plural in English]___

4. Mater <u>dona nova</u> adorabit. ___Mother will adore the new gifts.___

_____

Exercise B. Underline the direct object and its adjective if there is one. Translate.

1. The student carries a <u>small tablet</u>. ___Discipulus tabellam parvam portat.___

2. The students carry <u>large tablets</u>. ___Discipuli magnas tabellas portant.___

3. The kitchen has <u>a table</u> and <u>chair</u>. ___Culina mensam et sellam habet.___

4. The poet loves <u>the harp</u>. ___Poeta chitaram amat.___

5. The farmer sees <u>the shop</u>. ___Agricola tabernam videt.___

Derivatives. Complete sentences with derivatives from today's lesson.

1. ___Culinary___ means having to do with cooking and eating.

2. If you violate your ___conscience___ you will become hardened to sin.

3. ___Agriculture___ is the cultivation of the land.

4. ___Conscious___ means mentally awake and aware.

~ 36 ~

Lesson Plan VIII

SAYING

A useful expression for any teacher!

WORD STUDY

Ager is an agricultural field, *campus* is a field used for games, assemblies, etc. The first three words in this list are second declension masculine nouns that have *er* in the nominative singular instead of *us*. The genitive singular forms, *agri* and *libri,* drop the **e.** Our English words *agriculture, library,* and *magistrate* show the spelling of the stem, rather than the nominative form, and are a good way to help remember these words. These words illustrate again the reason for the important rule in the grammar section

Nota bene: *Gallia* and *Gallus. Gallia* is a country like *America, Gallus* is a person from that country like an *American.* The same thing applies to *Roma,* and *Romanus.*

Latin Saying

Magister dixit

The master has spoken

Vocabulary

1.	ager, agri	*field*
2.	liber, libri	*book*
3.	magister, magistri	*master, teacher*
4.	Gallus, i	*a Gaul*
5.	Romanus, i	*a Roman*
6.	vicus, i	*town, village*
7.	apostolus, i	*apostle*
8.	Christianus, i	*a Christian*
9.	lupus, i	*wolf*
10.	Marcus, i	*Mark*

Grammar Forms

Second Declension nouns ending in *er*

S.	Pl.
ager	agr-i
agr-i	agr-orum
agr-o	agr-is
agr-um	agr-os
agr-o	agr-is

Grammar

Once the stem is found by dropping the **i** from the genitive singular, these nouns are declined regularly.

> **Rule**
>
> The genitive singular is always used to
> (a) identify the declension
> (b) find the stem.

Sayings. Translate.

1. Retro Satana! _____ Get thee behind me, Satan. _____
2. Natura non facit saltum. _____ Nature does not make leaps. _____
3. Tibi gratias ago. _____ Thank you. _____

Drill A. Identify case and number. Translate using meanings from table.
Some words will have more than one answer.   [All 2nd declension]

1. vico _____ dat., abl. _____ sing. _____ to, for the village; by, with, from the village
2. apostoli _____ gen. sing; _____ nom. pl. _____ of the apostle, the apostles
3. Romanorum _____ gen. _____ pl. _____ of the Romans
4. Christianos _____ acc. _____ pl. _____ the Christians
5. libris _____ dat., abl. _____ pl. _____ to, for the books; by, with, from the books
6. lupum _____ acc. _____ sing. _____ the wolf

Drill B. Give the following forms.

1. *genitive singular*: sella, vicus _____ sellae _____ vici _____
2. *accusative plural*: villa, lupus _____ villas _____ lupos _____
3. *dative plural*: vita, agnus _____ vitis _____ agnis _____

Drill C. Decline.

1.		2.	
liber	libri	magister	magistri
libri	librorum	magistri	magistrorum
libro	libris	magistro	magistris
librum	libros	magistrum	magistros
libro	libris	magistro	magistris

(1) **CALL CARDS** for all masculine nouns, Lessons III, VIII

(2) Tape Form for today's vocabulary

(3) Exercises

(4) Study for quiz

DERIVATIVES

ager agri   *agriculture*

liber libri   *library*

magister, tri   *magistrate*
magisterium
(teaching office of the Catholic church)
majesty

vicus, i   *vicinity*

Lesson Plan VIII

Exercise A. Translate.

1. Lucia librum habet. _____ Lucy has a book. _____
2. Romani Gallos superant. ___ The Romans conquer the Gauls. ___
3. Agricola lupum non amat. ___ The farmer does not love the wolf. ___
4. Christiani Deum laudant. ___ Christians praise God. ___
5. Christus apostolos vocabat. _ Christ was calling the apostles. ___

Exercise B. Translate.

1. The lamb does not love the wolf. ___ Agnus lupum non amat. ___
2. The teacher was waiting for the students. _ Magister discipulos exspectabat. -
3. The Gauls will seize the village. ___ Galli vicum occupabant. ___
4. The books are new. _____ Libri sunt novi. _____

Derivatives. Give English derivatives for the first three words in today's lesson. From what form of the Latin word do the English derivatives come?

_____ agriculture, library, magistrate _____

_____ derived from the genitive form _____

_____

Lesson Plan VIII

Lesson Plan IX

SAYING

This is the education motto of the Jesuits, history's most famous and successful educators. Jesuit schools emphasized Latin and were unsurpassed in their reputation for excellence. This saying has great import for the study of Latin, because repetition and drill are so important in mastering this language or any language. The process of learning something new is often hard and unpleasant. The unfamiliar becomes familiar and loved *only* through repetition.

Latin Saying

Repetitio mater studiorum

Repetition is the mother of learning

Vocabulary

1.	periculum, i	*danger, peril*
2.	scutum, i	*shield*
3.	studium, i	*enthusiasm, zeal, learning*
4.	saeculum, i	*time, period, age, world*
5.	Evangelium, i	*Gospel*
6.	mandatum, i	*command, commandment*
7.	principium, i	*beginning, foundation*
8.	angelus, i	*angel*
9.	puer, pueri	*boy*
10.	vir, viri	*man, husband*

Grammar Forms

Second Declension nouns ending in *er, ir*

S.	Pl.
puer	puer-i
puer-i	puer-orum
puer-o	puer-is
puer-um	puer-os
puer-o	puer-is

Grammar

Remove the genitive singular ending, **i,** to find the stem *puer* and *vir.* The second declension masculine endings are then added regularly to the stems. Ask students to decline *vir.*

vir	**vir-i**
vir-i	**vir-orum**
vir-o	**vir-is**
vir-um	**vir-os**
vir-o	**vir-is**

Second declension nouns that end in *er* or *ir* are in two groups:

(1) magister, liber, ager: drop the e in the genitive.
(2) puer, vir: the nominative form is identical to the stem.

Sayings. Translate.

1. The master has spoken. _Magister dixit._

2. Nature does not make leaps. _Natura non facit saltum._

3. Get thee behind me, Satan! _Retro Satana._

4. Sicut erat in principio et nunc et semper et in saecula saeculorum.

   As it was in the beginning, is now and ever shall be, world without end.

5. Novus ordo seclorum. _New order of the ages._

Drill A. Identify case and number. Translate using meanings from table.
   Some words will have more than one answer.   [All 2nd declension]

1. pericula   nom., acc. pl.   dangers

2. angelorum   gen. pl.   of the angels

3. principio   dat., abl. sing   to, for the beginning; by, with, from the beginning

4. saeculum   nom., acc. sing.   age

5. studio   dat., abl. sing.   to, for learning; by, with, from learning

6. scuti   gen. sing.   of the shield

Drill B. Give the following forms.   [1=1st decl; 2=2nd decl.]

1. _genitive singular_: periculum, angelus, casa

   periculi [2]   angeli [2]   casae [1]

2. _dative singular_: scientia, Gallus, scutum

   scientiae [1]   Gallo [2]   scuto [2]

3. _ablative plural_: peccatum, vir, janua

   peccatis [2]   viris [2]   januis [1]

4. _nominative plural_: agricola, mandatum, puer

   agricolae [1]   mandata [2]   pueri [2]

WORD STUDY

Puer and _vir_ are two more 2nd decl. masculine nouns. _Vir_ means man as compared to woman; a male person, a man of courage. _Homo_ means man as compared to animals; man as a human being.

Related Latin words/sayings:

Novus ordo seclorum, (seclorum is a form of saeculum). _Sicut erat in principio, et nunc et semper et in saecula saeculorum._ (From the _Gloria Patri_)

ASSIGNMENT

CALL CARDS for all neuter nouns from today's lesson and Lesson III. Exercises and quiz as usual.

Ab Extra

Ab Extra:
Try translating these Bible verses.

In principio creavit Deus caelum et terram.
In the beginning God created the heaven and earth.

In principio erat Verbum et Verbum erat apud Deum et Deus erat Verbum.
In the beginning was the Word and the Word was with God and the Word was God.

Lesson Plan IX

DERIVATIVES

periculum, i   *peril*
                 perilous

scutum, i   *escutcheon (a shield on which a coat of arms is displayed)*

studium, i   *study*
                 student
                 studious
                 studio

saeculum, i   *secular*

Evangelium, i   *evangelist*
                 evangelical
                 evangelism

mandatum, i   *mandate*
                 mandatory

principium, i   *principle*
                 principal

angelus, i   *angelic*

puer, i   *puerile*

vir viri   *virtue*
                 virile
                 virtual
                 triumvirate

Exercise A. Translate.

1. Discipuli multos libros amant.   The students love many books.

2. Christus viros malos judicabit.   Christ will judge bad men.

3. Lupus pericula non timet.   The wolf does not fear dangers.

4. Deus mandata summa dat.   God gives the highest commandments.

Exercise B. Translate.

1. God loves girls and boys.   Deus puellas et pueros amat.
2. The soldier was carrying a large sword and a shield.   Miles magnum gladium et scutum portabat.
3. The angels have harps.   Angeli chitaras habent.
4. The Romans were warning the Gauls.   Romani Gallos monebant.

Derivatives. Complete these sentences with derivatives from today's lesson.

1. Something that is not optional is   mandatory   .
2. Something that is dangerous is   perilous   .
3. A man who is very masculine is   virile   .
4. An adult who acts childishly is   puerile   .
5. The head of a school is called a   principal   .
6. A rule or basic law is a   principle   .

Lesson Plan X

SAYING

Hannibal led his armies through the countryside of Italy for nine years, but he never had the siege equipment and resources necessary to take a well-fortified city like Rome. Nevertheless Romans rightly feared that Hannibal would soon be at their gates. Did nervous Roman mothers frantically call their children home with this cry? In our age we have had our own version, *The Russians are coming!*

WORD STUDY

All of these words are prepositions. *Ab* before a noun that begins with a consonant is shortened to *a*; before a noun that begins with a vowel it is *ab*. Similar to our use of *a* and *an*.

Latin Saying

Hannibal ad portas!
Hannibal at the gates!

Vocabulary

1.	a, ab	*from, away from,* prep. with abl.
2.	cum	*with,* prep. with abl.
3.	de	*from, down from,* prep. with abl.
4.	in	*in, on,* prep. with abl.
5.	sine	*without,* prep. with abl.
6.	in	*in, into, against,* prep. with acc.
7.	circum	*around, about,* prep. with acc.
8.	ad	*to, near, toward,* prep. with acc.
9.	per	*through,* prep. with acc.
10.	trans	*across,* prep. with acc.

Grammar

A preposition is a word that shows the relation between a noun (or pronoun) and another word in the sentence. Prepositions may indicate *direction, time, manner, means,* or *agent.* You may illustrate one of these, direction, by setting a book on a desk and writing on the board: *the book is on the desk. On* shows the relation between the *book* and *desk.* Put the book *under* the desk or *above* the desk and write these prepositional phrases on the board.

A prepositional phrase consists of the :

preposition + its object (and modifiers, if any)

above the desk   **under the desk**

above the old desk   **under the new desk**

Most of the prepositions in this lesson express *direction*.

Sayings. Translate.

1. Repetitio mater studiorum.   Repetition is the mother of learning.
2. The master has spoken.   Magister dixit.
3. Nature does not make leaps.   Natura non facit saltum.
4. Per Christum Dominum Nostrum. Amen.   Through Christ Our Lord, Amen.

5. ante bellum   before the war

Grammar

1. Define a *preposition*. Shows the relation of one noun (pronoun) to another.
2. In Latin the object of a preposition may be in what two cases?
   accusative , ablative
3. When the preposition *in* is followed by the accusative case it indicates
   motion .
4. When *in* is followed by the ablative case it indicates position .

Drill A. Translate.

1. cum amicis   with friends
2. trans agrum   across the field
3. per januam   through the door
4. in aqua   in the water
5. de caelo   down from heaven
6. a vicis   away from the villages
7. sine scientia   without knowledge
8. ad tabernas   toward the shops
9. trans culinam   across the kitchen

DERIVATIVES

The Latin prepositions *ab, cum* (*com*), *de, in, circum, ad, per, trans* are also common prefixes in English that have the same meanings as they do in Latin. Many words should come to mind as examples of English words with these Latin prefixes:

absent
absord
confort
commit
descend
deport
transport
admit
indent
circumnavigate
circumference
perfect
percussion

Grammar Cont.

Prepositions are used extensively in English, less so in Latin (which often uses the dative and ablative *without prepositions* to express these relations). However Latin does have prepositional phrases similar to English. *In Latin the object of the preposition may be in either the accusative or ablative case.* In English, of course, there is no objective case for nouns but we do put *pronouns* in the objective case when they are prepositional objects: *the book is under* him. *Him* is the objective case of the pronoun *he.*

In general prepositions whose meanings indicate *forward motion* take the accusative case: *trans, per, ad, circum, in,* whereas prepositions which indicate backward motion or no motion take the *ablative case*: *ab, cum, de, in, sine.*

The preposition *in* takes either case, depending on its meaning. If *in* means *location or place,* it takes the ablative.

In via sedet.   He is sitting in the road.

If *in* indicates forward motion (i. e. *into*), it takes the accusative case.

In silvam ambulat.   He walks into the forest.

Drill B. Translate.

1. through the shield   per scutum
2. without dangers   sine periculis
3. in the beginning   in principio
4. toward the wolf   ad lupum
5. into the village   in vicum
6. on the chair   in sella
7. across the province   trans provinciam
8. down from the farmhouse   de villa
9. away from the gate   a porta

Exercise A. Translate. Prepositional phrases are underlined.

1. Lucia <u>in villa</u> ambulat.   Lucy is walking in the farmhouse.

2. Marcus <u>in casam</u> ambulabat.   Mark was walking into the cottage.

3. Agricola <u>sine periculo</u> laborat.   The farmer works without danger.

4. Pueri et viri <u>circum mundum</u> navigant.   Boys and men sail around the world.

Exercise B. Translate. Prepositional phrases are underlined.

1. Farmers and poets live <u>in the village</u>.   Agricolae et poetae in vico habitant.

2. The boys are walking <u>with the girls</u>.   Pueri cum puellis ambulant.

3. The sailor sails <u>across the water.</u>   Nauta trans aquam navigat.

4. He is moving the chair <u>toward the table</u>.   Sellam ad mensam movet.

Grammar Cont.

Related Latin words/sayings:

Per *Christum Dominum Nostrum, Amen*. (Table blessing.)

Libera nos <u>a</u> malo (Pater Noster, a (ab), deliver us *from* evil).

In *Caelis,* in *caelo et* in *terra* (Pater Noster, *in* followed by the abl.).

In tentationem (Pater Noster, *in* followed by the acc. and indicating motion).

Prepositions should be learned in a prepositional phrase, if possible.

Ab Extra

Ab extra: *Cum laude*, with honors. *Dominus vobiscum*, the Lord be with you. *Cum* is often added to the end of the word that is its object. *Dominus tecum*, the Lord is with thee (Ave Maria).

Prepositions from BOOK I, *ante, contra, inter, post, supra*, take the acc.. *Ex* takes the abl., and *sub,* like *in* takes either the acc. or abl. depending on whether motion is indicated. Ante bellum, post mortem, post scriptum (P.S.).

Review Lesson B

Vocabulary

First declension nouns

		Prepositions
agricola, ae, *m.*	poeta, ae, *m.*	ab,a
ara, ae	porta, ae	cum
casa, ae	provincia, ae	de
cithara, ae	scientia, ae	in
culina, ae	sella, ae	sine
epistula, ae	tabella, ae	in
fabula, ae	taberna, ae	circum
janua, ae	tuba, ae	ad
Lucia, ae	umbra,ae	per
natura, ae	villa, ae	trans

Second declension nouns

	Masculine	*Neuter*
ager, agri	magister, magistri	Evangelium, i
angelus, i	Marcus, i	mandatum, i
apostolus, i	puer, pueri	periculum, i
Christianus, i	Romanus, i	principium, i
Gallus, i	vicus, i	saeculum, i
liber, libri	vir, viri	scutum, i
lupus, i		studium, i

Grammar Forms

Second Declension nouns ending in *er* or *ir*

S.	*Pl.*	*S.*	*Pl.*
ager	agr-i	puer	pueri
agr-i	agr-orum	pueri	puerorum
agr-o	agr-is	puero	pueris
agr-um	agr-os	puerum	pueros
agr-o	agr-is	puero	pueris

Latin Sayings

Retro Satana	Natura non facit saltum	Magister dixit
Repetitio mater studiorum	Hannibal ad portas!	

Assignment

Assign **CALL CARDS** for all 1st and 2nd declension nouns and prepositions from Lessons II- X. The tests in BOOK II do not include vocabulary from BOOK I, except as it occasionally appears in translation. However, you will want to include some of the BOOK I vocabulary on some quizzes and tests.

A good classroom assignment is to translate the Pater Noster. Make a copy without the pronunciation guide and with plenty of space underneath each word for students to write their translation. Students will be amazed at how many of the words they know or can figure out. Try to *parse* some words, that is, give the part of speech and declension, gender, case, part of sentence for nouns and adjectives, or conjugation, tense, person, number for verbs.

Assign the Doxology for memorization and translation. When translating, students should be given a copy that they can write the English word(s) beneath each Latin word. Students enjoy the accomplishment of being able to translate something real.

Drill A. Write each word in the case and number indicated. Translate.

		Case	Number		
1.	periculum	dat.	S.	periculo	to, for danger
2.	janua	gen.	Pl.	januarum	of the doors
3.	mandatum	abl.	Pl.	mandatis	by, with, from the commandments
4.	vir	dat.	Pl.	viris	to, for the men
5.	ager	gen.	Pl.	agrorum	of the fields
6.	casa	nom.	Pl.	casae	cottages
7.	saeculum	abl.	S.	saeculo	by, with, from the age
8.	puer	acc.	S.	puerum	boy
9.	scutum	acc.	Pl.	scuta	shields
10.	ara	acc.	Pl.	aras	altars

Drill B. Translate.

1.	in aquam	into the water	[1st, f., acc sg]
2.	with enthusiasm	cum studio	[2nd, n., abl sg]
3.	circum terram	around the earth	[1st, f., acc sg]
4.	near the Christians	ad Christianos	[2nd, m., acc pl]
5.	in casam	into the cottage	[1st, f., acc sg]
6.	around the chair	circum sellam	[1st, f., acc sg]

READING # 2
Roma et Carthago

Roma et Carthago sunt urbes [1]. Roma est in Italia. Carthago est in Africa.
Et Roma et[2] Carthago imperia habent. Carthago in Hispania et Sicilia imperium
habet. Roma in Italia imperium habet. Roma Carthaginem[3] non amat. Carthago
Romam non amat. Carthago multas naves[4] et servos habet. Carthago multam
pecuniam habet. Roma naves non habet. Roma agricolas et milites[5] habet.
Superabitne[6] Carthago Romam?

---
[1] nom. pl of *urbs*
[2] *et....et*, both....and
[3] acc. of *Carthago* (Carthage)
[4] acc. pl. of *navis*
[5] acc. pl of *miles*
[6] *ne* at end of first word in sentence indicates a question

Reading #2

Rome and Carthage are cities. Rome is in Italy. Carthage is in Africa. Both Rome and Carthage have empires. Cathage has command (an empire) in Spain and Sicily. Rome has command in Italy. Rome does not like Carthage. Carthage does not like Rome. Carthage has many ships and slaves. Carthage has much money. Rome does not have ships. Rome has farmers and soldiers. Will Carthage conquer Rome?

Lesson Plan XI

Present tense of *sum*

S.		Pl.	
sum	*I am*	sumus	*we are*
es	*you are*	estis	*you are*
est	*he, she, it is*	sunt	*they are*

Imperfect tense of *sum*

S.		Pl.	
eram	*I was*	eramus	*we were*
eras	*you were*	eratis	*you were*
erat	*he, she, it was*	erant	*they were*

Future tense of *sum*

S.		Pl.	
ero	*I will be*	erimus	*we will be*
eris	*you will be*	eritis	*you will be*
erit	*he, she, it will be*	erunt	*they will be*

Grammar

The forms in this lesson are the three tenses of the linking verb *to be*.

A linking verb is almost like an equal sign. It expresses *state of being*, not *action*.

Mark	is	a boy.		Mark	=	boy
sub.	*l.v.*	*pred. nom.*		predicate nominative		
Marcus	**est**	**puer**				
Mark	is	small		Mark	=	small
sub.	*l.v.*	*pred. adj.*		predicate adjective		
Marcus	**est**	**parvus**				

Exercise A. Underline the form of the "to be" verb in Latin. Translate sentence into English and underline the "to be" verb in English. Indicate whether it is a linking verb (l.v.) or a helping verb (h.v.). Write the number(s) of these found in each sentence:(1) predicate nominative (2) predicate adjective (3) direct object (4) prepositional phrase.

1. Marcus erat magister. _____ Mark was a teacher (lv) (1) _____

2. Lupi erant soli. _____ The wolves were alone. (lv) (2) _____

3. Galli in agris pugnabant. _____ The Gauls were fighting in the fields. (hv) (4) _____

4. Deus est summus. _____ God is highest. (lv) (2) _____

5. Liber in mensa erat. _____ A book was on the table. (lv) (4) _____

6. Viri erunt legati. _____ The men will be lieutenants. (lv) (1) _____

7. Marcus cum amicis ambulat. _ Mark is walking with friends. (hv) (4) _

8. Epistulae erunt longae. _____ The letters will be long. (lv) (2) _____

9. Apostoli Christianos in Roma appellabant. _____
   The apostles were addressing Christians in Rome. (hv) (3, 4)

10. Christus populum monebat. _ Christ was warning the people. (hv) (3) _

11. In horto servi erant. _____ Slaves were in the garden. (lv) (4) _____

12. Christus est Dominus. _____ Christ is Lord. (lv) (1) _____

Grammar Cont.

Predicate nominatives and predicate adjectives rename or describe the subject, and are therefore always in the nominative case. They always follow linking verbs. (Every sentence has two parts: a subject and a predicate. The subject is the thing or person that the sentence is about. The predicate makes an assertion about the subject and contains the verb.)

In English the forms of the verb *to be* (*am, is, are, was, were, will be*) are also helping verbs.

Marcus	is walking	through the fields.
sub.	a.v.	prep. phrase
Marcus	**ambulat**	**per agros.**

This sentence has an action verb *is walking* which consists of the main verb *walking* with a helping verb *is*. In this sentence *is* is a helping verb, not a linking verb. Students must learn to recognize when the forms of "to be" are linking verbs and when they are helping verbs.

Lesson Plan XI

Exercise B. Underline the form of the "to be" verb in English. Indicate whether it is a linking verb (l.v.) or a helping verb (h.v.). Translate sentence into Latin and underline "to be" verb in Latin (if there is one). Write the number(s) of these found in each sentence: (1) predicate nominative (2) predicate adjective (3) direct object (4) prepositional phrase.

1. Mark will be a soldier. Marcus erit miles. (lv) (1)
2. Mary is living in the farmhouse. Maria in villa habitat. (hv) (4)
3. The apostles were holy. Apostoli erant sancti. (lv) (2)
4. Caesar was a great general. Caesar erat magnus imperator. (lv) (1)
5. The farmer is in the field. Agricola est in agro. (lv) (4)
6. The soldier is my brother. Miles est frater meus. (lv) (1)
7. The farmers are moving the lambs into the field. Agricolae agnos in agrum movent. (hv)(3,4)
8. The shops are full. Tabernae sunt plenae. (lv) (2)
9. The harps are new. Citharae sunt novae. (lv) (2)
10. Lucy was washing the table in the kitchen. Lucia mensam in culina lavabat. (hv)(3,4)
11. The battle will be long. Proelium erit longum. (lv) (2)
12. The battles will be long. Proelia erunt longa. (lv) (2)

Exercise C. For each instruction write two sentences in English and two in Latin.

1. Linking verbs with predicate nouns.
   _____   _____
   _____   _____

2. Linking verbs with predicate adjectives.
   _____   _____
   _____   _____

3. Linking verbs with prepositional phrases.
   _____   _____
   _____   _____

4. Action verbs with helping verbs, *am, is, are, was* or *were*.
   _____   _____
   _____   _____

Grammar Cont.

The basic sentence patterns that will be used in this book are:

(1) Subject	verb	
(2) Subject	direct object *and/or* prepositional phrase	action verb
(3) Subject	linking verb	predicate nominative
(4) Subject	linking verb	predicate adjective
(5) Subject	linking verb	prepositional phrase

It must be remembered that word order in a Latin sentence is much more flexible than in English. The order presented in these models is not as important as the grammatical units. All nouns, of course, may be modified by adjectives.

Lesson Plan XII

SAYING

You will hear this saying often, once the students have realized its potential. Alexander Pope, an English essayist, critic, and poet of Enlightenment, added to it: *To err is human; to forgive, divine.*

WORD STUDY

First Conjugation verbs. The first verb, *voco*, is written with all of its *principal parts.*

Related Latin words/sayings:

Vox
vocis
specto
servus
In tentationem
(Pater Noster, tentatio, tentationis = temptation)

Latin Saying

Errare est humanum
To err is human
—Seneca

Vocabulary

1. voco, vocare, vocavi, vocatus — *call*
2. servo, are, avi, atus — *guard, keep*
3. aro, (1) — *plow*
4. exspecto, (1) — *wait for*
5. tempto, (1) — *tempt*
6. nato, (1) — *swim*
7. erro, (1) — *err*
8. saluto, (1) — *greet*
9. sto, stare, steti, status — *stand*
10. do, dare, dedi, datus — *give*

Grammar

The principal parts are those forms of a verb from which all of the other forms are derived. In English there are three principal parts:

Regular principal parts			Irregular principal parts		
infinitive	*past tense*	*past participle*			
to walk	walked	(have) walked	to be	was	(have) been
to kill	killed	(have) killed	to go	went	(have) gone
to clean	cleaned	(have) cleaned	to write	wrote	(have written

Lesson Plan XII

Sayings. Translate.

1. Repetition is the mother of learning. <u>Repetitio mater studiorum.</u>
2. Nature does not make leaps. <u>Natura non facit saltum.</u>
3. Da nobis hodie. <u>Give us today</u>
4. Magister dixit. <u>The master has spoken.</u>
5. Pray and work. <u>Ora et labora.</u>

Grammar

1. The forms from which all other verb forms are derived are called the <u>principal parts</u> .
2. The second principal part in Latin is called the <u>infinitive</u> .
3. In English the infinitive is always translated by the verb preceded by the preposition <u>to</u> .
4. Give the principal parts of
   - (a) nato <u>natare</u> <u>natavi</u> <u>natatus</u>
   - (b) porto <u>portare</u> <u>portavi</u> <u>portatus</u>
   - (c) laudo <u>laudare</u> <u>laudavi</u> <u>laudatus</u>

Drill A. Translate. [All 1st conjugation]

1. servabat <u>he, she, it was guarding</u> [3 sg imp]
2. erramus <u>we err</u> [1 pl pres]
3. eramus <u>we were</u> [1 pl imp]
4. natabimus <u>we will swim</u> [1 pl fut]
5. temptabant <u>they were tempting</u> [3 pl imp]
6. exspectabunt <u>they will wait for</u> [3 pl fut]
7. dabant <u>they were giving</u> [3 pl imp]
8. arant <u>they plow</u> [3 pl pres]

NOTA BENE:

(1) Small words such as *aro, erro* are easy to learn but are also easy to confuse with each other and other short words such as the future and imperfect forms of *sum,* or *ara, ae* (altar).

(2) Notice the spelling of *exspecto* differs from the English *expect*, without the *s*.

(3) In English the word *wait* is incomplete without the preposition *for,* but in Latin the sense of this preposition is included in the verb itself and it is incorrect to add the Latin word for *for.* This is similar to the verb *specto*, look at.

Grammar Cont.

In Latin most verbs have four principal parts, the first of which students will recognize as the form of the verb written in the vocabulary list, *the first person singular of the present tense.* The second principal part is called the *infinitive.* The infinitive expresses the pure form of the verb unassociated with any person or tense, "to call". In English, the infinitive is always preceded by the preposition "to". It is from the infinitive ending, *are,* that the stem vowel *a* originates. It is also the infinitive that classifies the verb according to conjugation.

> **Rule**
>
> Verbs whose infinitive ends in *are* are first conjugation verbs.

The third and fourth principal parts will be used in subsequent years to form additional tenses and forms of the verbs.

Lesson Plan XII

DERIVATIVES

voco	*vocation*
	vocal
	vocabulary
servo	*conserve*
	conservative
aro	*arable*
exspecto	*expectation*
tempto	*temptation*
nato	*natatorium (indoor swimming pool)*
erro	*errant*
	erratic
	aberration
saluto	*salutation*
	salute
sto	*stable*
	station
	status
do	*donate*
	donation
	donor

Drill B. Translate. [all 1st conjugation]

1. he will err ___errabit___ [3 sg fut]
2. we were swimming ___natabamus___ [1 pl imp]
3. they guard ___servant___ [3 pl pres]
4. you (s.) are giving ___das___ [2 sg pres]
5. he will tempt ___temptabit___ [3 sg fut]
6. you (pl.) will stand ___stabitis___ [2 pl fut]
7. he was plowing ___arabat___ [3 sg imp]
8. we will greet ___salutabimus___ [1 pl fut]
9. I was guarding ___servabam___ [1 sg imp]
10. you (pl.) were waiting for ___exspectabatis___ [2 pl imp]
11. it was tempting ___temptabat___ [3 sg imp]
12. they will stand ___stabunt___ [3 pl fut]

Exercise A. Translate.

1. Pueri parvum vicum servabunt.   ___The boys will guard the small village.___
2. Agricolae proximos agros arant.   ___The farmers are plowing (plow, do plow) the nearest fields.___
3. Viri feminas bonas exspectabant.   ___Men were waiting for the good women.___
4. Pueri et puellae in aqua natabant.   ___Boys and girls were swimming in the water.___
5. Marcus puellam in casa salutat.   ___Mark greets (does greet, is greeting) the girl in the cottage.___

Exercise B. Translate. Prepositional phrases are underlined.

1. Angels are guarding the door.   ___Angeli januam servant.___
2. Mother and Father are standing in the kitchen. ___Mater et Pater in culina stant.___
3. My son and my daughter are with friends. ___Filius meus et filia mea sunt cum amicis.___
4. Angels do not tempt boys and girls. ___Angeli pueros et puellas non temptant.___
5. The Romans do not fear danger and war. ___Romani periculum et bellum non timent.___

Grammar Cont.

Most verbs in the first conjugation have regular principal parts like *voco:*

voco, vocare, vocavi, vocatus

The stem is **voc** and the regular endings for the principal parts are: **o   are   avi   atus**

The (1) written after verbs 3-8 in the student book indicates that they are first conjugation verbs with regular principal parts, like *voco* and *servo.* The irregular principal parts of verbs, like sto and *do,* will be written out and must be memorized. All of the First conjugation verbs from Review Lesson I, except for *do,* have regular principal parts.

Principal parts of verbs may look intimidating to students, especially the irregular ones. The best way to learn them is to say them out loud. Like the declensions and conjugations, they should be learned as a unit, and repeated over and over. The principal parts of verbs in any language must be mastered thoroughly.

Lesson Plan XIII

SAYING

Traditionally it was the buyer who suffered the consequences for the shortcomings of the product he purchases. Today, because technology is so complicated, the government is taking a more active role in protecting the consumer. A *caveat* is a general warning to beware that something could be other than it seems.

WORD STUDY

Second conjugation verbs. The accent mark on the é of the infinitive is very important because it distinguishes the second conjugation from the third.

NOTA BENE

Caveo, like *exspecto* and *specto*, requires a preposition in English, *but not in Latin*, to complete its meaning.

Latin Saying

Caveat emptor
Let the buyer beware

Vocabulary

1.	moneo, monére, monui, monitus	*warn*
2.	placeo, ére, ui, itus	*please*
3.	valeo, valére	*am strong, am well*
4.	augeo, augére	*increase*
5.	caveo, cavére	*guard against, beware of*
6.	fleo, flére	*weep*
7.	rideo, ridére	*laugh*
8.	respondeo, respondére	*answer, reply*
9.	maneo, manére	*remain, stay*
10.	teneo, tenére	*hold*

Grammar

The endings for the regular principal parts of the second conjugation are those for *moneo*: *moneo, monére, monui, monitus.*

eo   ére   ui   itus

The infinitive ending ére provides the stem vowel é for the second conjugation.

> **Verbs whose infinitives end in ére belong to the second conjugation**

There are many verbs in the second conjugation with some irregularity in the 3rd and 4th principal parts. The only verbs which have regular principal parts in this lesson are *moneo* and *placeo*. Verbs 3-10 have irregular principal parts and will be learned later. In Review Lesson I, *terreo, habeo, debeo* and *prohi-*

Sayings. Translate.

1. To err is human. _____ Errare est humanum. _____
2. Valete. _____ Be well (Good-bye). _____
3. Vale magistra. _____ Good-bye, Teacher. _____
4. Rident stoldi verba Latina. Fools laugh at the Latin language.
5. Hannibal at the gates! _____ Hannibal ad portas! _____

Grammar

1. Verbs whose infinitive ends in *ére* belong to the ____second____ conjugation.
2. The endings for the regular principal parts of the second conjugation are
   ____ eo ére ui itus ____
3. Write the principal parts of
   (b) habeo ___habeo___ ___habére___ ___habui___ ___habitus___
   (c) debeo ___debeo___ ___debére___ ___debui___ ___debitus___

Drill A. Translate.   [All 2nd conjugation]

1. cavébit _____ he will guard against _____ [3 sg fut]
2. tenent _____ they hold _____ [3 pl pres]
3. placébunt _____ they will please _____ [3 pl fut]
4. ridet _____ he laughs _____ [3 sg pres]
5. flebant _____ they were weeping _____ [3 pl imp]
6. placébam _____ I was pleasing _____ [1 sg imp]
7. respondes _____ you answer _____ [2 sg pres]
8. augébis _____ you will increase _____ [2 sg fut]
9. valébimus _____ we will be well _____ [1 pl fut]
10. manétis _____ you remain _____ [2 pl pres]

DERIVATIVES

moneo	*monitor* *admonish*
placeo	*pleasant* *placid*
valeo	*valiant* *valuable*
augeo	*augment*
caveo	*caution*
fleo	*feeble*
rideo	*ridicule* *ridiculous*
respondeo	*respond* *response*
maneo	*mansion*
teneo	*tenant* *tenacious*

Lesson Plan XIII

Drill B. Translate.

1. they will remain _manebunt_
2. they were holding _tenebant_
3. we will answer _respondebimus_
4. she weeps _flet_
5. you (s) are well _vales_
6. we are laughing _ridemus_
7. he was staying _manebat_
8. you (pl) do increase _augetis_
9. I am replying _respondeo_
10. I will please _placebo_
11. I was guarding against _cavebam_
12. we will hold _tenebimus_

Exercise A. Translate.

1. Socii Romam cavent. _The allies guard against Rome._
2. Discipulus libros et epistulas tenebat. _The student was holding books and letter_
3. In horto manebit. _He will remain in the garden._
4. Pueri scientiam in ludo augebant. _The boys were increasing knowledge in school_
5. Servi flebant et ridebant. _The slaves were laughing and weeping._

Exercise B. Translate.

1. The farmer guards against the wolf. _Agricola lupum cavet._
2. The girls are warning the boys. _Puellae pueros monent._
3. A man will warn a friend. _Vir amicum monebit._
4. The boys and girls in the fields are laughing and crying.
   Pueri et puellae in agris rident et flent.

Derivatives. Use each derivative in a sentence.

1. tenacious _____
2. ridiculous _____
3. permanent _____
4. respond _____
5. valiant _____

Lesson Plan XIV

SAYING

The beginning of the Nicene Creed, recited in worship in many Christian churches. A meeting of all the bishops of the Church was called by Constantine in A.D. 325 in Nicaea, a city in Turkey, to deal with the Arian heresy about the divine nature of Christ. The creed is a summary of the most important doctrines of the Church and states in very clear language the triune nature of God and the divine and human nature of Jesus Christ.

Latin Saying

Credo in unum Deum

I believe in one God

Vocabulary

1.	ago, agere	*do, drive, act, treat*
2.	curro, currere	*run*
3.	duco, ducere, duxi, ductus	*lead, guide*
4.	bibo, bibere	*drink*
5.	rego, regere	*rule*
6.	pono, ponere, posui, positus	*put, place, set*
7.	trado, tradere	*deliver up, hand over*
8.	cado, cadere	*fall*
9.	credo, credere	*believe*
10.	vivo, vivere	*live*

Grammar Forms

Third conjugation present tense

rego	*I rule*	regimus	*we rule*
regis	*you rule*	regitis	*you rule*
regit	*he, she, it rules*	regunt	*they rule*

Grammar

The infinitive of the third conjugation ends in *ere* like the second, *but without the accent mark*.

> Verbs whose infinitive ends in *ere* belong to the third conjugation.

When learning these verbs it is very important to learn the second principal part along with the first, because in the *first principal part* these verbs are indistinguishable from the first conjugation.

	1st Conj.	2nd Conj.	3rd Conj.
1st Principal Part:	voco	moneo	ago
2nd Principal Part:	voc<u>a</u>re	mon<u>é</u>re	ag<u>e</u>re

Second conjugation verbs are easily remembered because the **e** is present in the first person singular, the form of the verb written in the vocabulary list. First and third conjugation verbs will be confused unless students know the infinitive of each verb as thoroughly as they know the first principal part.

Sayings. Translate.

1. Nature does not make leaps. ___Natura non facit saltum.___
2. Repetition is the mother of learning. ___Repetitio mater studiorum.___
3. Gratias tibi ago. ___Thank you.___
4. Miles Christi sum. ___I am a soldier of Christ.___
5. Quo vadis. ___Whither goest thou?___

Grammar

1. Verbs whose infinitive ends in **ere** belong to the ___third___ conjugation.
2. Give the principal parts of
   (a) **duco** ___duco___ ___ducere___ ___duxi___ ___ductus___
   (b) **pono** ___pono___ ___ponere___ ___posui___ ___positus___
3. Conjugate in the present tense:

   (a) **trado** ___trado___ ___tradimus___   (b) **curro** ___curro___ ___currimus___
   ___tradis___ ___traditis___   ___curris___ ___curritis___
   ___tradit___ ___tradunt___   ___currit___ ___currunt___

Drill A. Translate.   [All 3rd conjugation]

1. agis ___you do (drive, act)___
2. vivunt ___they live___
3. cadit ___he, she, it falls___
4. credis ___you believe___
5. ponitis ___you place___
6. bibimus ___we drink___
7. currunt ___they run___
8. ducis ___you lead___
9. regitis ___you rule___
10. tradit ___he, she, it hands over___
11. agunt ___they drive___
12. credimus ___we believe___

WORD STUDY

There are four conjugations in Latin, and these words belong to the THIRD CONJUGATION. *Habito* means to inhabit, dwell. *Vivo* means to live, be alive, to enjoy life.

Related Latin words, sayings:
dux, ducis;
rex, regis; regnum,
tibi gratias ago,
gratias agimus *tibi* (Gloria),
et ne nos inducas *in tentationem,*
(Pater Noster).
Vivat *academia,*
Vivant *professores, etc.,*
Et qui illam regit,
(Gaudeamus Igitur).

Nota Bene: *Trado, tradere* is a compound of *do* and the prefix *trans,* and like *specto* and *exspecto,* the preposition which in Latin is included in the verb, in English must be expressed separately.

Grammar Cont.

There is no model for principal parts in the third conjugation; each verb must be learned individually. However, students will begin to see patterns, so these verbs are not as difficult as they first appear.

The principal parts for *duco* and *rego* are given and should be committed to memory. The principal parts of the rest of these verbs will be learned later.

Since the infinitive of a third conjugation verb ends in *ere*, students will expect to see the *e* as the stem vowel in the present tense, but that is not the case. The mnemonic "Oh I Understand" may be helpful in remembering the variable stem vowel in the third conjugation present tense:

reg*o* (o)	reg*imus* (i)
reg*is* (i)	reg*itis* (i)
reg*it* (i)	reg*unt* (u)

Lesson Plan XIV

DERIVATIVES

ago   *agent*
                  agile

curro   *current*
                  currency
                  concurrent

duco   *duke*
                  duchess
                  abduct (ab+duco,
                  lead away from)
                  aqueduct
                  conduct

bibo   *bib*
                  beverage
                  imbibe

rego   *regal*
                  direct

pono   *exponent*
                  position
                  postpone

trado   *tradition*

cado   *cadence*
                  cascade

credo   *credible*
                  incredible
                  creed
                  credit

vivo   *revive*
                  vivid
                  revival

Educate is a compound of *ex* and *duco,* menaing to lead out of (of self).

Drill B. Translate.   [all 3rd conjugation]

1. he drinks   bibit   [3 sg pres]
2. we lead   ducimus [1 pl pres]
3. they hand over   tradunt [3 pl pres]
4. you (s.) live   vivis   [2 sg pres]
5. you (pl.) act   agitis   [2 pl pres]
6. I run   curro   [1 sg pres]
7. she is falling   cadit   [3 sg pres]
8. they do place   ponunt   [3 pl pres]
9. we are ruling   regimus   [1 pl pres]
10. you (s.) are leading   ducis [2 sg pres]
11. I am doing   ago   [1 sg pres]
12. it puts   ponit   [3 sg pres]

Exercise A. Translate. Prepositional phrases are underlined.

1. Pueri et puellae <u>in agro</u> currunt. _____
   The boys and girls run in the fields.
2. Libri et tabellae <u>de mensa alta</u> cadunt. _____
   Books and tablets fall from the high table.
3. Imperator magnam provinciam regit. _____
   The general rules a large province.
4. Legatus epistulas multas tradit.   The lieutenant hands over many letters.

Exercise B. Translate. Prepositional phrases are underlined.

1. Christ leads the apostles. _____ Christus apostolos ducit.
2. Mark is running <u>across the field</u>. _____ Marcus trans agrum currit.
3. They are placing the table <u>in the cottage</u>. Mensam in casa ponunt.
4. Lucy hands over the trumpets and harps. Lucia tubas et chitaras tradit.

Derivatives. Use each derivative in a sentence.

1. agent _____
2. conduct _____
3. incredible _____
4. cascade _____
5. revive _____

Lesson Plan XV

SAYING

The opening line of the *Aeneid*, the great epic poem written by Virgil during the reign of Augustus, the golden age of Roman literature. The *Aeneid* describes the wanderings of the Trojan hero, Aeneas, after the fall of Troy and his subsequent settlement in Latium. His descendants, of course, were the founders of Rome. The *Aeneid* was written to show that the Romans were destined by the gods for glory and greatness and that their ancestry goes back to the heroes of Troy, and to the gods themselves, since Aeneas's mother was the goddess Venus. The Romans, befitting their greatness, felt the necessity of an epic as great as the Illiad, the national epic of the Greeks and so Virgil produced this masterpiece of Latin for the emperor and the people of Rome. Traditionally it has been read in the third or fourth year of Latin study. Virgil is considered the greatest of the Roman poets.

Latin Saying

Arma virumque cano

I sing of arms and a man

—1st line of *Aeneid*

Vocabulary

1. defendo, defendere — *defend*
2. vinco, vincere, vici, victus — *conquer*
3. edo, edere — *eat*
4. tollo, tollere — *raise (up), take away*
5. cano, canere — *sing*
6. mitto, mittere, misi, missus — *send*
7. scribo, scribere — *write*
8. dico, dicere — *say, tell*
9. claudo, claudere — *shut, close*
10. peto, petere — *seek, beg*

Grammar Forms

Third conjugation imperfect tense

regebam	*I was ruling*	regebamus	*we were ruling*
regebas	*you were ruling*	regebatis	*you were ruling*
regebat	*he, she, it was ruling*	regebant	*they were ruling*

Grammar

The imperfect of the third conjugation follows the pattern of the first and second conjugations. The **e** from the infinitive *ere* appears as the stem vowel.

Lesson Plan XV

Sayings. Translate.

1. Veni, vidi, vici. _____ I came, I saw, I conquered. _____
2. Agnus Dei, qui tollis peccata mundi. _____
   _____ Lamb of God, who takes away the sins of the world. _____
3. Magister dixit. _____ The master has spoken. _____
4. Let the buyer beware. _____ Caveat emptor. _____
5. I believe in one God. _____ Credo in unum Deum. _____

Grammar

1. On blank paper conjugate in the present and imperfect tenses: (a) **vinco** (b) **tollo**
2. Give the principal parts of
   (a) **vinco**   vinco _____ vincere _____ vici _____ victus _____
   (b) **mitto**   mitto _____ mittere _____ misi _____ missus _____

Drill A. Translate.   [All 3rd conjugation]

1. petis _____ you seek _____ [2 sg pres]
2. dicit _____ he, she, it says _____ [3 sg pres]
3. edunt _____ they eat _____ [3 pl pres]
4. edebant _____ they were eating _____ [3 pl imp]
5. canebatis _____ you were singing _____ [2 pl imp]
6. tollebam _____ I was raising up _____ [1 sg imp]
7. scribunt _____ they write _____ [3 pl pres]
8. scribebant _____ they were writing _____ [3 pl imp]
9. defendebamus _____ we were defending _____ [1 pl imp]
10. vincitis _____ you conquer _____ [2 pl pres]
11. mittebas _____ you were sending _____ [2 sg imp]
12. canit _____ he, she, it sings _____ [3 sg pres]
13. scribebat _____ he, she, it was writing _____ [3 sg imp]
14. tollunt _____ they raise up _____ [3 pl pres]
15. petebat _____ he, she, it was seeking _____ [3 sg imp]

Word Study

More third conjugation verbs. Again two verbs are written with their complete principal parts.

Related Latin words/sayings:
Veni, vidi, vici.
Agnus Dei, qui tollis peccata mundi. Dimitte, dimittimus
(Pater Noster) are forms of dimitto: a compound of mitto
which means to send away or dismiss.
Christus vincit. Cantet nunc Io (Adeste fidelis).
(Both *canto* and *cano* mean sing.)

DERIVATIVES

defendo	*defensive*
	defense
	defendant
vinco	*convict*
	invincible
edo	*edible*
tollo	*tolerance*
cano	*canticle*
	cantata
mitto	*mission*
	missionary
	emit
	omit
	admit
	transmit
	submit
	permit
scribo	*scribe*
	describe
	postscript (p.s.)
	scripture
	scribble
dico	*dictionary*
	dictator
	predict
	verdict
	contradict
claudo	*clause*
	close
	closet
	claustrophobia
peto	*petition*

Lesson Plan XV

Drill B. Translate.   [all 3rd conjugation]

1. I was singing _____ canebam _____ [1 sg imp]
2. you (s.) were conquering _____ vincebas _____ [2 sg pres]
3. they are writing _____ scribunt _____ [3 pl pres]
4. she does eat _____ edit _____ [3 sg pres]
5. we were closing _____ claudebamus _____ [1 pl imp]
6. you (pl.) are sending _____ mittitis _____ [2 pl pres]
7. they were begging _____ petebant _____ [3 pl imp]
8. you (s.) take away _____ tollis _____ [2 sg pres]

Exercise A. Translate.

1. Apostoli multas et sanctas epistulas scribebant. _____
   The apostles were writing many holy letters. _____
2. Christus peccata tollit. _____ Christ takes away sins. _____
3. Angeli cum citharis et tubis canunt. _____ The angels sing with harps and trumpets.
4. Romani barbaros in Gallia vincebant. _____ The Romans were conquering the
   _____ barbarians in Gaul. _____

Exercise B. Translate.

1. The farmers and poets were eating and drinking in the shop. _____
   Agricolae et poetae in taberna edebant et bibebant. _____
2. Mark was closing the door. _____ Marcus januam claudebat. _____
3. The barbarians are defending Gaul. _____ Barbari Galliam defendunt. _____
4. The apostles were writing the Gospels. _____
   Apostoli Evangelia scribebant. _____

Derivatives. Use each derivative in a sentence.

1. dictionary _____
2. edible _____
3. missionary _____
4. petition _____
5. canticle _____

Review Lesson C

Grammar Forms

First conjugation verbs

aro, (1)
do, dare, dedi, datus
erro, (1)
exspecto, (1)
nato, (1)
saluto, (1)
servo, (1)
sto, stare, steti, status
tempto, (1)
voco, (1)

Second conjugation verbs

augeo, augére
caveo, cavére
fleo, flére
maneo, manére
moneo, monére
placeo, placére
respondeo, respondére
rideo, ridére
teneo, tenére
valeo, valére

Irregular verb *sun*

Present tense

S.	Pl.
sum	sumus
es	estis
est	sunt

Imperfect tense

eram	eramus
eras	eratis
erat	erant

Future tense

ero	erimus
eris	eritis
erit	erunt

Third conjugation verbs

ago, agere	edo, edere
bibo, bibere	mitto, mittere, misi, missus
cado, cadere	peto, petere
cano, canere	pono, ponere, posui, positus
claudo, claudere	rego, regere
credo, credere	scribo, scribere
curro, currere	tollo, tollere
dico, dicere	trado, tradere
defendo, defendere	vinco, vincere, vici, victus
duco, ducere, duxi, ductus	vivo, vivere

Third conjugation

Present tense

rego	regimus
regis	regitis
regit	regunt

Imperfect tense

regebam	regebamus
regebas	rebebatis
regebat	regebant

Latin Sayings

Errare est humanum	caveat emptor
Credo in unum Deum	Arma virumque cano

Assignment

Assign CALL CARDS for all verbs, including those from Book I. Verbs should <u>always</u> be said with their infinitive forms. Verbs should be drilled until students know them without hesitation. Assign the **Ave Maria** and/or **Sanctus** or **Gloria** for translation and memorization. Students should be learning music and memorization selections by singing and recitation every week.

Review Lesson C

Drill A. Check the correct tense, number, and person. Translate.

	Tense			Number		Person			Meaning
	Pres.	Fut.	Imp.	S.	Pl.	1	2	3	
1. arabimus		X			X	X			we will plow
2. stabit		X		X				X	he will stand
3. natas	X			X			X		you swim
4. valebunt		X			X			X	they will be well
5. ridet	X			X				X	he is laughing
6. augebam			X	X		X			I was increasing
7. eritis		X			X		X		you will be
8. currebat			X	X				X	he was running
9. tradebas			X	X			X		you were handing over
10. cadebant			X		X			X	they were falling
11. vivis	X			X			X		you live
12. vincunt	X				X			X	they conquer
13. dicebas			X	X			X		you were saying
14. petimus	X				X	X			we seek
15. edebamus			X		X	X			we were eating
16. dabo		X		X		X			I will give
17. servabitis		X			X		X		you will guard
18. scribebatis			X		X		X		you were writing

READING # 3
Lucia et Marcus

Lucia et Marcus in Italia habitabant. Lucia et Marcus in villa in Neapole[1] habitabant. Marcus et Lucia soror et frater erant. Marcus clamabat et pugnabat. Lucia orabat et canebat. Lucia a Marco currebat. Lucia ad villam currebat. Mater et pater in culina cum amicis edebant et bibebant. Lucia per culinam ad agros currebat. Servi in agris arabant. Pastores[2] lupos cavebant. Lucia trans agros ad casam currebat. Magister in casa pueros et puellas docebat. Discipuli in tabellis scribebant. Lucia circum casam currebat ad vicum. Populi in vico ridebant et flebant quod[3] poetae fabulas narrabant. Lucia in sella in taberna sedebat. Lucia erat sola et laeta[4]. Marcus Luciam videt! Marcus eam[5] salutat et sedet. Misera[6] Lucia!

[1] Naples
[2] shepherds
[3] because
[4] happy
[5] her
[6] poor (wretched)

Reading #3

Lucy and Mark were living in Italy. Lucy and Mark lived (were living) in a fram house in Naples. Mark and Lucy were brother and sister. Mark was shouting and fighting. Lucy was praying and singing. Lucy was running away from Mark. Lucy was running to the farmhouse. Mother and father were eating and drinking in the kitchen with friends. Lucy (ran) was running through the kitchen toward the fields. The slaves were plowing in the fields. The shepherds were guarding against wolves. Lucy was running across the fields toward a cottage. A teacher was teaching boys and girls in the cottage. Students were writing on tablets. Lucy (ran) was running around the cottage toward the village. People in the village were laughing and weeping because poets were telling stories. Lucy was sitting on a chair in the shop. Lucy was alone and happy. Mark sees Lucy. Mark greets her and sits (down). Poor Lucy.

~ 73 ~

Lesson Plan XVI

SAYING

The words of the gladiators as they entered the arena for mortal combat; a line students may feel appropriate as they enter the classroom for a particularly difficult test.

WORD STUDY

These words belong to the FOURTH CONJUGATION.

> ### RULE
>
> Verbs whose infinitive ends in *ire* belong to the fourth conjugation.

Related Latin words/sayings:

Veni, vidi, vici,
Benedictus qui venit (Sanctus),
Veni Creator spiritus,
Veni, Veni Emmanuel,
Venite adoremus (Adeste Fideles),
scientia, ae

Latin Saying

> **Ave Caesar - morituri te salutamus**
>
> **Hail Caesar - we who are about to die salute you**
>
> -- Roman gladiators

Vocabulary

1.	audio, audire, audivi, auditus	*hear*
2.	dormio, ire, ivi, itus	*sleep*
3.	munio, (4)	*fortify, construct*
4.	impedio, (4)	*hinder, impede*
5.	scio, (4)	*know*
6.	finio, (4)	*finish, end, limit*
7.	punio, (4)	*punish*
8.	venio, venire	*come*
9.	aperio, aperire	*open*
10.	sentio, sentire	*feel, perceive, think*

Grammar Forms

Fourth conjugation present tense

audio	*I hear*	audimus	*we hear*
audis	*you hear*	auditis	*you hear*
audit	*he, she, it hears*	audiunt	*they hear*

Grammar

Most of these verbs have regular principal parts like *audio*: *audio, audire, audivi, auditus*. The regular endings for the principal parts are:

io   ire   ivi   itus

Second and fourth conjugation verbs are easily distinguished in their first principal parts because the stem vowel is present.

voco   mon<u>e</u>o   rego   aud<u>i</u>o

For verbs like *voco* and *rego* it is especially important to learn infinitives in order to remember what conjugation the verbs belong to, e.g. *voco, voc<u>are</u>; rego, reg<u>ere.</u>*

Sayings. Translate.

1. Veni, vidi, vici. _____ I came, I saw, I conquered. _____
2. I sing of arms and a man. _____ Arma virumque cano. _____
3. To err is human. _____ Errare est humanum. _____
4. The mother of Italy - Rome. _____ Mater Italiae - Roma _____

Grammar

1. Verbs whose infinitives end in **ire** belong to the _____ fourth _____ conjugation.
2. Give the principal parts of
   (a) **munio** _____ munio _____ munire _____ munivi _____ munitus _____
   (b) **scio** _____ scio _____ scire _____ scivi _____ scitus _____
3. Conjugate in the present tense :

venio	venimus	impedio	impedimus
venis	venitis	impedis	impeditis
venit	veniunt	impedit	impediunt

Drill A. Translate. [All 4th conjugation]

1. finis — you finish — [2 sg pres]
2. venit — he, she, it comes — [3 sg pres]
3. dormiunt — they sleep — [3 pl pres]
4. punitis — you punish — [2 pl pres]
5. sentimus — we feel — [1 pl pres]
6. sciunt — they know — [3 pl pres]
7. aperit — he, she, it opens — [3 sg pres]
8. punimus — we punish — [1 pl pres]
9. auditis — you hear — [2 pl pres]
10. impedis — you impede — [2 sg pres]
11. munit — he, she, it fortifies — [3 sg pres]
12. muniunt — they fortify — [3 pl pres]

DERIVATIVES

audio	audition, auditorium, audible, audience
dormio	dormitory, dormant, dormer
munio	ammunition, munitions
impedio	impediment
scio	science, conscience, conscious
finio	final, finite
punio	punitive
venio	advent, intervene, event
aperio	aperture
sentio	sensitive, resent, sentimental, sentiment

Grammar Cont.

The present tense of the fourth conjugation is similar to the third, except that *the stem vowel,* i*, is present in the 1st person singular and the 3rd person plural.* The same three vowels appear in the present tense, *IOU*.

Lesson Plan XVI

Drill B. Translate.

1. We are fortifying ___munimus___
2. I am coming ___venio___
3. You (s.) do know ___scis___
4. They are finishing ___finiunt___

5. He does open ___aperit___
6. You (pl.) sleep ___dormitis___
7. He is feeling ___sentit___
8. They hinder ___impediunt___

Exercise A. Translate.

1. Viri ad portam dormiunt. _____
   _____ Men sleep at the gate. _____

2. Pueri et viri fabulas audiunt. _____
   _____ Boys and men hear stories. _____

3. Puella januam aperit. ___The girl opens the door.___

4. Discipulus tabellam finit. ___The student finishes the tablet.___

5. Romani in Galliam veniunt. ___The Romans are coming into Gaul.___

Exercise B. Translate.

1. The poets know many stories. ___Poetae multas fabulas sciunt.___
2. The Romans are punishing the Gauls. ___Romani Gallos puniunt.___
3. You are impeding knowledge. ___Scientiam impedis.___
4. The farmer is coming around the cottage. ___Agricola circum casam venit.___

Derivatives. Use each derivative in a sentence.

1. impede _____
2. auditorium _____
3. dormitory _____
4. Advent _____
5. punish _____

Lesson Plan XVII

WORD STUDY

Latin has many adverbs and conjunctions which are not particularly memorable, but must be learned nevertheless. It is helpful to learn them in expressions which are memorable, or make up a useful nonsense phrase to aid memory. *Hodie mihi, cras tibi.* Today for me, tomorrow for thee. A favorite with students: *Semper ubi sub ubi.* Always wear underwear.

Ab extra: *Ex nihilo nihil fit.* Nothing can be made out of nothing. The Greek philosophers and the Romans after them believed that the world could not have been made out of nothing and thus was eternally existent. Jewish and Christian tradition have always interpreted Genesis to mean that God created the universe *ex nihilo*, out of nothing; God is eternally existent, but matter had a beginning in time.

Latin Saying

Hodie Christus natus est

Today Christ is born

Vocabulary

1.	hodie	*today, this day*
2.	cras	*tomorrow*
3.	heri	*yesterday*
4.	quod	*because*
5.	quis	*who?*
6.	quid	*what?*
7.	ubi	*where?*
8.	cur	*why?*
9.	sed	*but*
10.	nihil	*nothing*

Grammar Forms

Fourth conjugation imperfect tense

audiebam	*I was hearing*	audiebamus	*we were hearing*
audiebas	*you were hearing*	audiebatis	*you were hearing*
audiebat	*he, she, it was hearing*	audiebant	*they were hearing*

Grammar

The imperfect of the fourth conjugation has the regular imperfect endings preceded by the two vowels **ie**. The third and fourth conjugations are similar and should be learned in comparison to each other. This will become more evident when the *future tense* of these two conjugations is learned later.

Sayings. Translate.

1. Hail Caesar - we who are about to die salute you. _____

   Ave Caesar, morituri te salutamus.

2. The Roman peace. _____ Pax Romana.

3. The voice of the people is the voice of god. _ Vox populi, Vox dei. _

4. Get thee behind me, Satan. _____ Retro Satana. _

5. Repetition is the mother of learning. ___ Repetitio mater studiorum. _

Grammar

1. Conjugate in the present and imperfect tenses

dico	dicimus	**dormio**	dormimus
dicis	dicitis	dormis	dormitis
dicit	dicunt	dormit	dormiunt

dicebam	dicebamus	dormiebam	dormiebamus
dicebas	dicebatis	dormiebas	dormiebatis
dicebat	dicebant	dormiebat	dormiebant

Drill A. Translate.

1. Hodie veniunt. _____ Today they are coming. _

2. Heri veniebant. _____ Yesterday they were coming. _

3. Hodie dicis. _____ Today you are saying. _

4. Heri dicebas. _____ Yesterday you were saying. _

5. Hodie dormit. _____ Today he is sleeping. _

6. Heri dormiebat. _____ Yesterday he was sleeping. _

7. Hodie finimus. _____ Today we are finishing. _

8. Heri finiebamus. _____ Yesterday we were finishing. _

Lesson Plan XVII

Drill B. Translate.

1. Tomorrow we will weep. (*fleo*) _____ Cras flebimus.
2. Today we are writing. (*scribo, scribere*) _____ Hodie scribimus.
3. Yesterday he was opening. (*aperio*) _____ Heri aperiebat.
4. Tomorrow you (s.) will err. (*erro, errare*) _____ Cras errabis.
5. Today he is plowing. (*aro, arare*) _____ Hodie arat.
6. Yesterday they were plowing. _____ Heri arabant.
7. Tomorrow he will guard. (*servo, servare*) _____ Cras servabit.
8. Today I am laughing. (*rideo*) _____ Hodie rideo.

Exercise A. Translate.

1. Quid agis? _____ What are you doing?
2. Poetas amo quod fabulas narrant. _____
   _____ I love poets because they tell stories.
3. Librum amo quod bonus est. _____ I like the book because it is good.
4. Cur rides? _____ Why are you laughing?
5. Ubi es? _____ Where are you?
6. Agricola agrum arabat sed poeta canebat. _____
   _____ The farmer was plowing the field but the poet was singing.
7. Quid auditis? Nihil audimus. _____
   _____ What do you hear? We hear nothing.

Exercise B. Translate.

1. Why are you writing on the tablet? _____ Cur in tabella scribis?
2. Who is plowing? _____ Quis arat?
3. Who is in the kitchen? _____ Quis est in culina?
4. What is he eating? _____ Quid edit?
5. Where is the lamb? _____ Ubi est agnus?

Lesson Plan XVIII

LATIN SAYING

Christ chose as his emissaries to the world, not those clothed in the greatness and power of Rome, but the simple and humble fishermen of Galilee. St. Augustine wrote *Civitas Dei*, the *City of God*, in A.D. 430, while Rome was falling to the invasion of the barbarians. In this work he contrasted the City of Man, exemplified by Rome, and the true city destined for immortality and greatness, the City of God. The City of God consists of those who follow the way of Christ, and it has its visible expression in the supranational organization, the Church.

WORD STUDY

Students should recognize these nouns as more of the third declension nouns learned last year. Since the genitive form has to be learned also, this list may look formidable, but because many of the nouns are so similar to English and they change in such predictable ways, this vocabulary list should pose no problems. Invite students to make observations.

Latin Saying

Non oratorem, non senatorem, sed piscatorem.

Not an orator, not a senator, but a fisherman.

--St. Augustine

Vocabulary

1. clamor, clamoris — *shouting, shout*
2. orator, oratoris — *speaker, orator*
3. senator, senatoris — *senator*
4. mos, moris, *m.* — *custom*
5. timor, timoris — *fear*
6. volúntas, voluntátis — *will, good will*
7. pastor, pastoris — *shepherd*
8. virgo, virginis — *virgin*
9. lectio, lectionis — *lesson*
10. piscator, piscatoris — *fisherman*

Grammar Forms

Third declension

Masc. and Fem.

S.	Pl.
lex	leg-es
leg-is	leg-um
leg-i	leg-ibus
leg-em	leg-es
leg-e	leg-ibus

Grammar

In the third declension, masculine and feminine nouns are declined the same way. The declension of third declension nouns should be practiced in class until you are sure students understand how to (1) find the stem and (2) add the endings. The genitive singular form provides the stem, *leg*. Find the stem for all of the words in the vocabulary list: *clamor, orator, senator, mor, timor, voluntat, pastor, virgin, lection, piscator.*

Rule

All nouns whose genitive singular ends in *is* belong to the third declension.

Gender: *In the third declension there are no characteristic endings to distinguish gender, as there are in the first two declensions. Each word has to be learned individually.* Several rules can help in learning the gender of these nouns, however, and will be taught in the next few lessons. All gender rules have exceptions *except* for the first one.

Lesson Plan XVIII

Sayings. Translate.

1. The Senate and People of Rome_____
   Senatus Populusque Romanus

2. Fiat voluntas tua.   Thy will be done.

3. Hail Caesar - we who are about to die, salute you._____
   Ave Caesar, morituri te salutamus.

Grammar   *Words like hostis and canis that can refer to either a male or female are called common gender, c, and can be either masculine or feminine gender.

1. Nouns whose genitive singular ends in *is* belong to the ___third___ declension.

2. What is the *natural gender rule*? What declensions does it apply to? _____
   names of male persons are masculine, of female persons feminine - all declensions

3. Applying the *natural gender rule*, what nouns in today's lesson are masculine?
   orator, senator, pastor, piscator   Feminine?   virgo

4. Applying the *natural gender rule*, what nouns in Lesson IV are masculine? *____
   frater, pater, centurio, Caesar, imperator, miles, rex, homo Feminine?   mater, soror

5. Applying the *natural gender rule*, what first declension nouns are masculine?
   nauta, poeta, agricola

6. Applying the *masculine endings rule*, which words in today's lesson are masculine? _
   clamor, timor
   In Lesson IV ?   dolor

7. On blank paper, decline: (a) **mos** (b) **pastor** (c) **miles** (d) **piscator** (e) **clamor**

Drill A. Give the accusative singular and plural in Latin.[All 3rd declension]

1. shepherd   pastorem, pastores
2. shout   clamorem, clamores
3. lesson   lectionem, lectiones
4. virgin   virginem, virgines
5. fisherman   piscatorem, piscatores
6. will, good will   voluntatem, voluntates

WORD STUDY Cont.

Pastor, senator, clamor, and *orator* are the same as our English words. Along with *clamor, piscator,* and *timor* the change in form from the nominative to the genitive is *or* -*oris*. Other English words with the *or* ending are *actor, debtor, etc.* Remember that the letter *g* is soft before *e* and *i* and hard before *a , o* and *u*.

Related Latin words/sayings:

Pisces,
virgo,
clamo clamare,
oro orare,
timeo timére.
Senatus Populusque Romanus,
Fiat voluntas *tua* (Pater Noster).
In the declension of *lex*, students have heard the *ibus* ending from *debitoribus* in the Pater Noster.

Grammar Cont.

3rd Declension Gender Rule #1

Natural Endings
Words naming male persons are masculine; words naming female persons are feminine. There are no exceptions to this rule and it is always applied before any other rule, and applies to all declensions.

Rex, frater, pater, imperator, miles, senator, orator, pastor, piscator, centurio, homo are all *masculine*. *Poeta, nauta*, and *agricola* are *masculine* even though they are first declension nouns. Women had few occupations outside of the home, so any word describing a traditionally male role would be masculine.

Some words like *hostis* or *civis*, can refer either to a male or female and are indicated common gender, *c*.

Ask students to pick out third declension words that are feminine from last year's words in Lesson IV and this lesson: *mater, soror, virgo.*

Lesson Plan XVIII

DERIVATIVES

clamor	*clamor*
	clamorous
	exclamation
orator	*orator*
	oratorio
	oratory
mos	*moral*
timor	*timorous*
	timid
	intimidate
voluntas	*voluntary*
pastor	*pastoral*
lectio	*lecture*

Drill B. Translate. [all 3rd declension]

1. with the shepherds _____ cum pastoribus _____ [m., abl pl]
2. to/for the senator _____ senatori _____ [m., dat sg]
3. without the shepherd _____ sine pastore _____ [m., abl. sg]
4. in the lessons _____ in lectionibus _____ [f., abl. pl]
5. of the fears _____ timorum _____ [m., gen pl]
6. to/for the customs _____ moribus _____ [m., dat pl]
7. by/with/from the shouts _____ clamoribus _____ [m., abl pl]
8. toward the fishermen _____ ad piscatores _____ [m., acc. pl]

Exercise A. Translate.

1. Christus piscatores vocabat. _____
   Christ was calling the fishermen.
2. Pastor agnos ducit. The shepherd leads the lambs.
3. Quid senatores in foro dicebant? _____
   What were the senators in the forum saying?
4. Discipuli lectiones parabunt. _____
   The students will prepare lessons.
5. Romani agricolae erant, non piscatores. _____
   The Romans were farmers, not fishermen.

Exercise B. Translate.

1. Fears impede the people. (*impedio*) Timores populum impediunt.
2. Customs guide the people. (*duco*) Mores populum ducunt.
3. He was walking with the shepherd. Cum pastore ambulabat.
4. The Virgin is holy. Virgo est sancta.
5. Mark hears the shouts. Marcus clamores audit.

Grammar

3rd Dec. Gender Rule #2

Masculine Endings
Most words that have these endings are masculine.

or oris
tor toris

In the vocabulary lists, the gender of words with these endings will not be given *unless they are exceptions*. What words in today's vocabulary are masculine according to this rule? *clamor, timor*

Lesson Plan XIX

LATIN SAYING

Cato ended every speech in the Senate with these words. Eventually Rome followed his advice and utterly destroyed her mortal enemy, Carthage, sowing the ground with salt.

WORD STUDY

Students should start to see patterns in the changes from nominative to genitive forms.

> io - ionis
> tas - tatis
> or - oris
> x - cis
> x - gis

According to *Natural Gender Rule*, what is the gender of *dux* and *custos*?

Related Latin words/sayings:

Tempto, temptare
duco, ducere
libero, liberare
Panem nostrum cotidianum; et ne nos inducas in *tentationem* (Pater Noster).

Latin Saying

> **Delenda est Carthago**
>
> **Carthage must be destroyed**
>
> —Cato the Elder

Vocabulary

1.	panis, panis, *m.*	*bread*
2.	custos, custodis	*guard*
3.	tentatio, tentationis	*temptation*
4.	pes, pedis, *m.*	*foot*
5.	dux, ducis	*leader*
6.	libertas, libertatis	*freedom, liberty*
7.	arbor, arboris, *f*	*tree*
8.	sol, solis, *m.*	*sun*
9.	caritas, caritatis	*love, charity*
10.	passio, passionis, *f.*	*suffering*

Grammar Forms

Third declension Case Endings

Masc. and Fem.

S.	Pl.
--	es
is	um
i	ibus
em	es
e	ibus

Grammar

By the third declension students may start to confuse the different endings and feel overwhelmed. An index card containing all of the endings organizes the Latin declensions for students and makes the task appear much less intimidating. After all, anything that can be contained on an index card can't be all that difficult to learn! Students can use the card as a handy reference until they are confident without it. On a 3x5 or 4x6 card, draw one horizontal and three vertical lines and use each block for a set of endings. Add the endings in the top four blocks and the bottom left block as shown below. (The bold **i** in the genitive plural, 3rd decl., will not be added until lesson 20.) When the card is finished at the end of the year, students will feel a great sense of accomplishment and also feel they have a "handle" on the declensions.

Lesson Plan XIX

DERIVATIVES

Sayings. Translate.

1. Not an orator, not a senator, but a fisherman. Non oratorem, non senatorem, sed piscatorem

2. I sing of arms and a man. ___ Arma virumque cano. ___

3. Nature does not make leaps. ___ Natura non facit saltum. ___

4. I believe in one God. ___ Credo in unum Deum. ___

Grammar

1. Applying the **natural gender rule**, which words in today's lesson are masculine?
   ___ custos, dux ___ Are any feminine? ___ no ___

2. Are any words in today's lesson masculine according to the **masculine endings** rule?
   ___ no ___ Which word is an exception? ___ arbor ___

3. Applying the **feminine endings** rule, which words in today's lesson are feminine?
   ___ tentatio, libertas, caritas ___ In Lesson XVIII ? ___ voluntas, lectio ___
   In lesson IV ? ___ civitas, veritas, virtus ___

4. On blank paper, decline: **panis, arbor, dux, tentatio, custos**

Drill A. Give case and number, translate. [All 3rd declension]

1. duce	ablative	sing.	by, with, form the leader
2. custodi	dative	sing.	to, for the guard
3. panem	accusative	sing.	bread
4. solum	genitive	pl.	of the suns
5. caritate	ablative	sing.	by, with, from love
6. tentationibus	dat., abl.	pl.	to, for; by, with, from temptations
7. pedum	genitive	pl.	of the feet
8. arborum	genitive	pl.	of the trees

DERIVATIVES

panis	*pantry*
	*companion**
custos	*custody*
	custodian
tentatio	*temptation*
pes	*pedal*
	centipede
	pedestrian
	impede
	impediment
dux	*duke*
	duchess
	aqueduct
arbor	*arboretum*
	arbor

*com-panion means: *together with* + *bread.* Breaking bread with someone is an act of friendship, fellowship.

DERIVATIVES CONTINUED ON NEXT PAGE

Grammar Cont.

1st decl. F.		2nd. decl. M.		2nd. decl. N.		Cases	Use
S.	Pl.	S.	Pl.	S.	Pl.		
a	ae	us	i	um	a	Nom.	sub.
ae	arum	i	orum	i	orum	Gen.	poss.
ae	is	o	is	o	is	Dat.	I.O.
am	as	um	os	um	a	Acc.	D.O.
a	is	o	is	o	is	Abl.	by/with/from

3rd decl. M/ F.		3rd decl. N		4th decl.		5th decl.	
S.	Pl.	S.	Pl.	S.	Pl.	S.	Pl.
—	es	—	a	us	us	es	es
is	ium	is	um	us	uum	ei	erum
i	ibus	i	ibus	ui	ibus	ei	ebus
em	es	—	a	um	us	em	es
e	ibus	e	ibus	u	ibus	e	ebus

Lesson Plan XIX

DERIVATIVES CONT.

sol   *solar*
                solstice
                parasol

caritas   *care*
                charity

passio   *passion*

Drill B. Translate.

1. without suffering   sine passione
2. in the trees   in arboribus
3. to/for bread   pani
4. of leaders   ducum
5. temptations   tentationes
6. toward liberty   ad libertatem
7. across the sun   trans solem
8. around the feet   circum pedes

Exercise A. Translate.

1. Lucia panem in mensa ponit.
    Lucy places bread on the table.
2. Christus libertatem dat.
    Christ gives liberty.
3. Luna circum terram movet.
    The moon moves around the earth.
4. Terra circum solem movet.
    The earth moves around the sun.
5. Custodes januas claudebant.
    The guards were closing the doors.

Exercise B. Translate.

1. The trees move in the wind.   Arbores in vento movent.
2. The apostles were having temptations and sufferings.
    Apostoli tentationes et passiones habebant.
3. The leaders and senators praise liberty.
    Duces et senatores libertatem laudant.
4. The sun was moving across the sky.   Sol trans caelum movebat.

      * caelum is neuter in the singular, masculine in the plural

Derivatives. Use each derivative in a sentence.

1. solar
2. companion
3. pedal
4. custodian

Grammar

The gender of words that observe this rule will not be given in vocabulary lists.

Legio is a word like ship, city, or nation. Even though a ship may have only men it is still considered feminine, even in English. *Legio* and *passio* have the endings *io-ionis*, which is not the same as *tio-tionis*. Both words, however, are feminine.

> ### 3rd Dec. Gender Rule #3
>
> **Feminine Endings**
> Words with these endings are usually feminine.
>
> **tas - tatis**
> **tus - tutis**
> **tudo - tudinis**
> **tio - tionis**

Lesson Plan XX

SAYING

Roman citizens had rights and protections that other subjects of the empire did not possess. Even St. Paul valued his Roman citizenship and used it to secure a trial after he was arrested. The conditions of his imprisonment were pleasant compared to the usual treatment of Christians. Eventually he met his death by beheading, rather than the horrible death of crucifixion, suffered by most of the other apostles. The feeling of Roman citizens moving about the empire must have been similar to the feelings of Americans as we travel about the world. Most governments are very concerned for the safety of the lives of American citizens, fearing to incur the wrath of the American government. Because the best of the ideals of *Aeterna Roma* are part of the foundation of western civilization, we can say proudly with St. Paul and others throughout history, *I am a citizen of Rome.*

Latin Saying

Romanus civis sum

I am a citizen of Rome

Vocabulary

1.	avis, avis, *f.*	*bird, sign, omen*
2.	ovis, ovis, *f.*	*sheep*
3.	orbis, orbis, *m.*	*world, orbit, circle*
4.	mens, mentis, *f.*	*mind, understanding*
5.	ars, artis, *f.*	*art, skill*
6.	nix, nivis, *f.*	*snow*
7.	finis, finis, *m.*	*end, boundary*
8.	dens, dentis, *m.*	*tooth*
9.	sedes, sedis, *f.*	*seat, abode*
10.	civis, civis, *m. or f.*	*citizen*

Grammar Forms

Third declension *i-stem* nouns

S.	*Pl.*
pars	part-es
part-is	part-<u>ium</u>
part-i	part-ibus
part-em	part-es
part-e	part-ibus

Grammar

Pars, partis, part, is a third declension noun from Book I. What is the difference between this declension and the previous one? There is an *i* in the genitive plural. All of the nouns in today's lesson have this *i* in the genitive plural and are called *i-stems*. This will not pose any problem to students if it is presented as a *little irregularity* found in the third declension. Have students put a red *i* before the genitive plural ending on their index card to remind them that some third declension nouns have this irregularity. *I-stem* nouns can be M, F, or N.

3rd Decl. M/F:	*S.*	*Pl.*
	-	es
	is	ium
	i	ibus
	em	es
	e	ibus

Words from Book I that are also i-stems are *hostis, urbis, ignis, collis, navis, nox, gens, mons, mors, pars*. In general these words are one or two syllables and often have the same number of syllables in both the nominative and genitive forms, *hostis, avis, finis, sedes, civis, orbis, etc.* It is not necessary for students to remember which nouns are *I-stems* this year or to overemphasize this lesson, since the genitive is not used this year.

Sayings. Translate.

1. Today Christ is born. ___Hodie Christus natus est.___
2. Carthage must be destroyed. ___Delenda est Carthago.___
3. Let the buyer beware. ___Caveat emptor.___
4. In the year of Our Lord. ___Anno Domini___

Grammar

1. Third declension nouns that have an **i** in the genitive plural are called ___i-stem___.
2. On blank paper, decline: **dens, sedes, ovis**
3. On blank paper, decline (a) **bad leader** (b) **good law**

Drill A. Translate.   [All 3rd declension]

1. cum civibus ___with the citizens___
2. in nive ___in snow___
3. circum orbem ___around the world___
4. sine arte ___without skill___
5. dentes ___teeth___
6. sedes ___seats (nom pl. & acc pl.) seat (nom. sing.)___
7. avium ___of the birds___
8. ovi ___to, for the sheep___
9. mente ___by, with, from the mind___
10. finem ___end___
11. civium ___of the citizens___
12. avi ___to, for the bird___

WORD STUDY
Another pattern for third declension words is *ns - ntis*.

Related Latin words/sayings:
> *sedeo,*
> *civitas,*
> *finio finire.*
> Mentes *tuorum visita*
> (Veni Creator Spiritus).

DERIVATIVES

avis	*aviation*
	aviator
	aviary
orbis	*orbit*
mens	*mental*
ars	*artist*
	artificial
finis	*finish*
	definite
dens	*dental*
	dentist
sedes	*sedentary*
	sedimentary
civis	*civil*
	civilian
	civilization

Grammar Cont.

Third declension nouns and 1st/2nd declension adjectives.

The adjectives learned last year and listed in lesson V are called 1st/2nd declension adjectives because they are declined exactly like the nouns from the first two declensions. But what if a third declension noun is modified by a 1st/2nd declension adjective? How would you say *good leader* or *good law*? Leader, *dux,* is a 3rd declension masculine noun and *good* is a 1st/2nd declension adjective which must agree with its noun in *gender*, *number*, and *case*. Therefore, *good leader* is *dux bonus* and *good law* is *lex bona.*

Good leaders are fighting in the battle.	**Duces boni in proelio pugnant.**
The senators write good laws.	**Senatores leges bonas scribunt.**

The declensions of *good leader* and *good law* are:

S.	Pl.	S.	Pl.
dux bonus	duces boni	lex bona	leges bonae
ducis boni	ducum bonorum	legis bonae	legum bonarum
duci bono	ducibus bonis	legi bonae	legibus bonis
ducem bonum	duces bonos	legem bonam	leges bonas
duce bono	ducibus bonis	lege bona	legibus bonis

Lesson Plan XX

Drill B. Translate.

1. many birds _multae aves_
2. small sheep _parvae oves (parva ovis)_
3. of the arts _artium_
4. of the birds _avium_

5. with the sheep _cum ovibus (ove)_
6. by/with/from the seat _sede_
7. toward the end _ad finem_
8. the great minds _magnae mentes_

Exercise A. Translate.

1. Cives in nive cadunt. _The citizens are falling in the snow._
2. Aves dentes non habent. _Birds do not have teeth._
3. Pastores oves ducebant. _The shepherds were leading the sheep._
4. Quid oratores dicunt? _What are the orators saying?_
5. Poetae cum arte canunt. _Poets sing with skill._

Exercise B. Translate.

1. The shepherds were defending the sheep.
   Pastores oves defendebant.
2. The citizens were always looking at birds.
   Cives aves semper spectabant.
3. Snow is falling down from the sky. _Nix de caelo cadit._
4. The boy has a bad tooth. _Puer dentem malum habet._

Derivatives. Use each derivative in a sentence.

1. aviation
2. artistic
3. dental
4. civil
5. mental

Grammar

Review Lesson D

Fourth conjugation verbs	Other words	Fourth conjugation present tense	
aperio, aperire	cras	audio	audimus
audio, (4)	cur	audis	auditis
dormio, (4)	heri	audit	audiunt
finio (4)	hodie		
impedio, (4)	nihil	**imperfect tense**	
munio, (4)	quid		
punio, (4)	quis	audiebam	audiebamus
scio, (4)	quod	audiebas	audiebatis
sentio, sentire	sed	audiebat	audiebant
venio, venire	ubi		

Third declension nouns
masculine and feminine

		"ium" nouns
arbor, arboris, *f.*	passio, passionis, *f.*	ars, artis, *f.*
caritas, caritatis	pastor, pastoris	avis, avis, *f.*
clamor, clamoris	pes, pedis, *m.*	civis, civis, *c.*
custos, custodis	piscator, piscatoris	dens, dentis, *m.*
dux, ducis	senator, senatoris	finis, finis, *m.*
lectio, lectionis	sol, solis, *m.*	mens, mentis, *f.*
libertas, libertatis	tentatio, tentationis	nix, nivis, *f.*
mos, moris *m.*	timor, timoris	orbis, orbis, *m.*
orator, oratoris	virgo, virginis	ovis, ovis, *f.*
panis, panis, *m.*	voluntas, voluntatis	sedes, sedis, *f.*

Third declension noun forms
Case endings
masculine and feminine

S.	Pl.	S.	Pl.		S.	Pl.
lex	leges	-	es		pars	partes
legis	legum	is	**(i)um**		partis	part**ium**
legi	legibus	i	ibus		parti	partibus
legem	leges	em	es		partem	partes
lege	legibus	e	ibus		parte	partibus

Latin Sayings

Ave Caesar, morituri te salutamus
Romanus civis sum
Non oratorem, non senatorem, sed piscatorem

Hodie Christus natus est
Delenda est Carthago

Assignment

Assign **Call Cards** for all words in this Review Lesson. When students have mastered the vocabulary (0 cards in the left stack), they should practice spelling the Latin words either orally or written, when going from English to Latin. To know a Latin noun means to know its *spelling*, *declension* and *gender*. To know a Latin verb means to know its *spelling*, *conjugation*, and *principal parts* (if given).

Continue to work on memorized passages and music.

Drill A. Give the correct form of the verb. Translate.

		Tense	Person	Number		
1.	venio	pres.	3	S.	venit	he is coming
2.	finio	imp.	2	Pl.	finiebatis	you were finishing
3.	munio	pres.	1	Pl.	munimus	we fortify
4.	punio	imp.	3	Pl.	puniebant	they were punishing
5.	scio	pres.	2	S.	scis	you know

Drill B. Give the nominative and genitive singular and gender.

1.	tooth	dens	dentis	m.
2.	fear	timor	timoris	m.
3.	lesson	lectio	lectionis	f.
4.	freedom	libertas	libertatis	f.
5.	suffering	passio	passionis	f.
6.	bread	panis	panis	m.
7.	seat	sedes	sedis	f.
8.	mind	mens	mentis	f.
9.	guard	custos	custodis	m.
10.	sun	sol	solis	m.

READING # 4
Caesar

Galli et Romani semper pugnabant. Galli erant barbari. Romani erant cives. Senatus Populusque Romanus Caesarem in Galliam mittebant. Caesar Gallos puniebat quod trans finem provinciae[1] veniebant. Caesar et milites in Galliam veniebant. Caesar Romam et imperium Romanum defendebat. Galli fortes[2] erant sed Caesar eos[3] vincebat. Galli magnum ducem habebant sed Caesar eum[4] vincebat. Caesar ad Britianniam[5] navigabat sed Britianniam non vincebat. Caesar autem[6] imperator summus erat. Caesar orator et imperator et scriptor[7] magnus erat. Laudasne[8] Caesarem?

---

[1] boundary of the province
[2] brave
[3] them
[4] him
[5] Britain
[6] however
[7] writer
[8] ne at end of first word of sentence indicates a question

Reading #4

Gauls and Romans were always fighting. The Gauls were barbarians. The Romans were citizens. The Senate and People of Rome were sending Caesar into Gaul. Caesar was punishing the Gauls because they were coming across the boundary of the province. Caesar and the soldiers were coming (came) into Gaul. Caesar was defending Rome and the Roman empire (Romanus can also be an adjective). The Gauls were brave but Caesar was conquering them. The Gauls were having (had) a great leader but Caesar was conquering him. Caesar was sailing toward Britain but he was not conquering Britain. However, Caesar was the greatest general. Caesar was a great orator, general and writer. Do you praise Caesar?

Lesson Plan XXI

SAYING

Cicero opened his famous speech in the Senate against Catiline with *How long will you abuse our patience, Catiline*, and then he exclaimed, *O tempora, O mores.* This is the classic expression for those who want to bemoan the conditions of their own culture.

WORD STUDY

All of the words in today's lesson are neuter, except for *sal, salis* which is masculine.

[Note: *mare* is an i-stem noun; the genitive plural is *marium.*]

Latin Saying

O tempora, O mores

O the times, O the customs

—Cicero

Vocabulary

1.	iter, itineris, *n.*	*journey, march, route*
2.	vulnus, vulneris	*wound*
3.	sal, salis *m.*	*salt, sea water*
4.	mare, maris	*sea*
5.	carmen, carminis, *n.*	*song*
6.	cor, cordis, *n.*	*heart*
7.	rus, ruris	*countryside*
8.	ver, veris, *n.*	*spring (season)*
9.	opus, óperis	*work, deed*
10.	flumen, fluminis, *n.*	*river*

Grammar Forms

Third declension neuter

S.	Pl.
flumen	flumin-a
flumin-is	flumin-um
flumin-i	flumin-ibus
flumen	flumin-a
flumin-e	flumin-ibus

Grammar

Invite students to compare the declension of these nouns with second declension neuters. Neuter nouns always have the same nominative and accusative endings in both the singular and the plural. The vowel *a* is the plural ending in these two cases, as it was in the second declension.

> **Gender - The Neuter Endings Rule:** *3rd decl.* nouns that end in these letters are usually neuter.
>
> **US**
> **E**
> **EN**
> **AR**

The gender of words that observe this rule will not be given in the vocabulary lists.

Lesson Plan XXI

Sayings. Translate.

1. I am a citizen of Rome. _____ Romanus civis sum.
2. Hannibal at the gates! _____ Hannibal ad portas!
3. Not an orator, not a senator, but a fisherman. _____
   _____ Non oratorem, non senatorem, sed piscatorem.
4. Work conquers all. Labor omnia vincit.

Grammar

1. Applying the **neuter endings** rule, which words in today's lesson are neuter ?
   _____ all but sal _____ In Lesson IV? _____
   _____ caput, tempus, flumen, nomen, corpus
2. On blank paper, decline: **carmen**, **vulnus**, **opus**, **cor**, **miles** (masc.)
3. On blank paper, decline (a) **deep river** (b) **long journey**

Drill A. Give the accusative singular and plural. [All 3rd declension]

1. flumen _____ flumen, flumina _____   3. opus _____ opus, opera _____
2. cor _____ cor, corda _____   4. vulnus _____ vulnus, vulnera _____

Drill B. Translate.   [nouns all 3rd declension]

1. magnum opus _____ great work _____
2. plenum cor _____ full heart _____
3. multa carmina _____ many songs _____
4. trans rus _____ across the countryside _____
5. per flumina _____ through the rivers _____
6. vulnere _____ by, with, from a wound _____
7. sine multis vulneribus _____ without many wounds _____
8. in sale _____ in salt _____

DERIVATIVES

iter	*itinerary*
vulnus	*vulnerable*
	invulnerable
sal	*saline*
mare	*marine*
	maritime
	submarine
cor	*cordial*
	core
	courage
rus	*rural*
ver	*vernal*
opus	*operator*
	operation
flumen	*fluid*

ASSIGNMENT

Assign CALL CARDS for all third declension neuter words, Lessons IV, and XXI.

Lesson Plan XXI

Drill C. Translate.

1. to/for the hearts _____cordibus_____
2. journeys _____itinera_____
3. in the deep river _____in alto flumine_____
4. through the deep river _____
   _____per altum flumen_____
5. in the deep sea _____in alto mare_____
6. of the good songs _carminum bonorum_
7. of the good song _carminis boni_
8. to/for the new works _____
   _____operibus novis_____

Exercise A. Translate.

1. Iter est longum. _____The journey is long._____
2. Vulnera erant mala. _____The wounds were bad._____
3. Milites trans multa flumina veniebant. _____
   _____The soldiers were coming across many rivers._____
4. Milites multa vulnera habent sed pugnant. _____
   _____The soldiers have many wounds but are fighting._____
5. Multi milites sunt in itinere. _____
   _____Many soldiers are on the march. ··_____

Exercise B. Translate.

1. The poet sings without heart. _____Poeta sine corde canit._____
2. The poets sing many songs. _____Poetae multa carmina canunt._____
3. The soldiers are fighting in the river. _____
   _____Milites in flumine pugnant. ··_____
4. The boys and girls are waiting for spring. _____
   _____Pueri et puellae ver exspectant._____

Derivatives. Use each derivative in a sentence.

1. rural _____
2. invulnerable _____
3. itinerary _____
4. cordial _____

Lesson Plan XXII

SAYING
Even the smallest action has consequences, casts a shadow.

WORD STUDY
All of these words except for the three nouns are adverbs. They are often some of the most difficult words to learn because they usually are not related to English words and the meanings are easily confused. I think the best way to learn them is to say the words aloud with the English meaning immediately afterwards. Many students learn a pun or some trick to help bring the meaning to mind.

Vocabulary

1.	undique	*on (from) all sides*
2.	statim	*at once, immediately*
3.	os, oris, *n.*	*mouth*
4.	itaque	*therefore*
5.	autem	*however*
6.	etiam	*also, even*
7.	tum	*then, at that time*
8.	jus, juris, *n.*	*right*
9.	diu	*for a long time*
10.	fons, fontis, *m.* (i-stem)	*fountain, spring, source*

fons is an i-stem noun
(see Lesson XX for i-stems)

Latin Saying

Etiam capillus unus habet umbram

Even one hair has a shadow

—Publius Syrus

Grammar Forms

CASE ENDINGS
Third declension neuter

S.	Pl.
--	a
is	um
i	ibus
--	a
e	ibus

Grammar

Add these endings to student index card. Only two more blocks to fill and students will have learned all of their declensions!

Sayings. Translate.

1. O the times, O the customs   O tempora, O mores
2. my fault   mea culpa
3. I am a citizen of Rome   Romanus civis sum.
4. wonder of the world   stupor mundi

Grammar

1. In Latin, neuter nouns of any declension, singular and plural, always have the same endings for what two cases?   nominative , accusative
2. On blank paper, decline: **fons, jus, os**

Drill A. Translate.

1. jura   rights   [3rd decl.]
2. fontium   of the fountains   [3rd decl.]
3. oribus   to, for; by, with, from mouths   [3rd decl.]
4. diu   for a long time
5. undique   from all sides
6. etiam   also
7. juribus   to, for; by, with, from the rights   [3rd decl.]
8. fonti   to, for the fountain   [3rd decl.]

Drill B. Give the following forms.   [1, 2, 3 = declension]

1. *dative singular*: amicus amico [2] , os ori [3] ,
   panis pani [3] , stella stellae [1] ,
   gaudium gaudio [2]
2. *genitive singular*: ventus venti [2] , puella puellae [1] ,
   jus juris [3] , lex legis [3] , studium studii [2]
3. *ablative plural*: puer pueris [2] , casa casis [1] ,
   mandatum mandatis [2], fons fontibus [3] , timor timoribus [3]

DERIVATIVES

os
oral
orifice

jus
jury
just
injure

fons
font
fount

Lesson Plan XXII

Exercise A. Translate.

1. Tum milites undique veniebant. _____

   At that time the soldiers were coming from all sides.

2. Senatores timores multos habent, manent autem. _____

   The senators have many fears, however they are staying.

3. Etiam fons aquam non habet. _____

   Even the fountain does not have water.

4. Magister docebat, discipulus autem os aperiebat. _____

   The teacher was teaching, however the student was opening (his) mouth.

Exercise B. Translate.

1. Immediately the general seeks peace. _____

   Statim imperator pacem petit.

2. The citizens seek peace, however the generals prepare war. _____

   Cives pacem petunt, imperatores autem bellum parant.

3. The fountains will have much water. _____

   Fontes multam aquam habebant.

4. The guards were standing at the gates for a long time. _____

   Custodes ad portas diu stabant.

Derivatives. Use each derivative in a sentence.

1. oral _____
2. jury _____
3. juror _____
4. fountain _____

Lesson Plan XXIII

SAYING

Satire from Cicero. The scriptures also speak of wolves in sheep's clothing. It is often the sad state of affairs that the very men we need to be protected from are, in fact, put in authority over us.

WORD STUDY

Like some English words, the singular and plural of these 4th declension words cannot be distinguished in the nominative (sheep). Fourth declension words are masculine unless otherwise indicated. The fourth and fifth declensions are very small, containing few words.

Related Latin words/sayings:
equus,
porta (gate),
Senatus Populusque Romanus,
venio.

Latin Saying

O praeclarum custodem ovium lupum.

O, excellent protector of sheep, the wolf.

—Cicero

Vocabulary

1.	adventus, us	*coming, arrival*
2.	equitatus, us	*cavalry*
3.	exercitus, us	*army*
4.	portus, us	*harbor*
5.	senatus, us	*senate*
6.	spiritus, us	*spirit*
7.	fructus, us	*fruit, profit, enjoyment*
8.	usus, us	*use, experience*
9.	lacus, us	*lake, pit*
10.	impetus, us	*attack*

Grammar

Fourth Declension

Noun Forms

S.	Pl.
port-us	port-us
port-us	port-uum
port-ui	port-ibus
port-um	port-us
port-u	port-ibus

Case Endings

S.	Pl.
us	us
us	uum
ui	ibus
um	us
u	ibus

Grammar

This declension is easy, *u* being the dominant vowel. Add these endings to student index card and look forward to the 5th and last declension next week.

Sayings. Translate.

1. Even one hair has a shadow. _____Etiam capillus unus habet umbram._____
2. Gloria Patri et Filio et Spiritui Sancto _____
   Glory to the Father, Son, and the Holy Ghost
3. always faithful _____semper fidelis_____
4. I sing of arms and a man. _Arma virumque cano._

Grammar

1. Nouns whose genitive singular ending is *us* belong to the declension. _fourth_
2. Most fourth declension nouns are _masculine_ in gender.
3. On a separate piece of paper, decline: (a) **equitatus** (b) **usus** (c) **deep lake**

Drill A. Give the accusative singular and plural of these fourth declension nouns.

1. fructus _____fructum_____ _____fructus_____
2. equitatus _____equitatum_____ _____equitatus_____
3. usus _____usum_____ _____usus_____
4. impetus _____impetum_____ _____impetus_____

Drill B. Translate. [All 4th declension]

1. fructuum _____of the fruits_____ [gen pl]
2. adventum _____arrival_____ [acc sg]
3. portibus _____to, for; by, with, from the harbors_____ [dat, abl pl]
4. sine equitatu _____without the cavalry_____ [abl sg]
5. a lacu _____away from the lake_____ [abl sg]
6. de portu _____down from the harbor_____ [abl sg]
7. ad exercitum _____toward the army_____ [acc sg]
8. impetum _____attack_____ [acc sg]
9. in spiritu _____in the spirit_____ [abl sg]
10. cum senatu _____with the senate_____ [abl sg]
11. lacibus _____to, for; by, with, from the lakes_____ [dat, abl pl]
12. usibus _____to, for; by, with, from the experiences_____ [dat, abl pl]

DERIVATIVES

adventus	*advent*
	adventure
equitatus	*equestrian*
exercitus	*exercise*
portus	*port*
	seaport
spiritus	*spiritual*
fructus	*fruit*
impetus	*impetuous*

Lesson Plan XXIII

C. Translate.

1. around the lake ___circum lacum___
2. through the harbors ___per portus___
3. into the cavalry _____
    ___in equitatum___
4. with the army ___cum exercitatu___

5. of the harbors ___portuum___
6. to/for the arrival ___adventui___
7. by/with/from experience _____
    ___usu___
8. across the lake ___trans lacum___

Exercise A. Translate.

1. Imperator exercitum circum lacum ducebat. _____
    The general was leading the army around the lake.
2. Senatus adventum expectabit. _____
    The Senate will wait for the arrival.
3. Agricolae fructus ad portum portabunt. _____
    The farmers will carry fruit to the harbor.
4. Imperator impetum prohibebat. _____
    The general was preventing the attack.

Exercise B. Translate.

1. The army is coming near Carthage. _____
    Exercitus ad Carthaginem venit.
2. The cavalry is coming from all sides. ___Equitatus undique venit.___
3. Christ sends the Holy Spirit. ___Christus Spiritum Sanctum mittit.___
4. The general leads the large army. _____
    Imperator magnum exercitum ducit.

Derivatives. Use each derivative in a sentence.

1. impetuous _____
2. advent _____
3. adventure _____
4. equestrian _____

Lesson Plan XXIV

SAYING

The *Dies Irae* is a beautiful and famous hymn (a good college dictionary will have an entry for *Dies Irae*) from the Middle Ages that is sung in the Requiem Mass (funeral Mass). It describes the day of judgment and implores God for mercy. The *Dies Irae* has been a favorite of composers because of its dramatic qualities and beauty. Mozart's Requiem Mass is the most famous and is performed often by Choral groups, much like Handel's Messiah. The mysterious circumstances surrounding the commission of this Mass by a stranger and Mozart's death before its completion add to the mystique of this much performed work. This story is retold in the contemporary movie *Amadeus,* which does have a beautiful sound track, containing some of the *Dies Irae,* even though the portrayal of Mozart is disappointing.

Latin Saying

Dies Irae

Day of Wrath

Vocabulary

1. dies, diei, *m.*	*day*
2. acies, ei	*battle line*
3. fides, ei	*faith, loyalty*
4. res, ei	*thing*
5. spes, ei	*hope*
6. meridies, ei, *m.*	*midday, noon*
7. facies, ei	*face*

Grammar

Fifth Declension

Noun Forms			Case Endings	
S.	*Pl.*		*S.*	*Pl.*
r-es	r-es		es	es
r-ei	r-erum		ei	erum
r-ei	r-ebus		ei	ebus
r-em	r-es		em	es
r-e	r-ebus		e	ebus

Grammar

Add these endings to the final block in student index cards and have a celebration.

This passage from I Cor. 13: 12-13 may provide a good classroom exercise in translation. Read aloud from an English translation and then let students copy the Latin and match English and Latin words.

Videmus	**nunc**	**per**	**speculum**	**in enigmate,**	**tunc**	**autem**	**facie**	**ad**	**faciem.**
We see	*now*	*through*	*mirror*	*in darkness*	*then*	*however*	*face*	*to*	*face.*

Nunc	**cognosco**	**ex parte,**	**tunc**	**autem**	**cognoscam**	**sicut**	**et**	**cognitus sum.**
Now	*I know*	*from(in) part,*	*then*	*however*	*I will know*	*as*	*(also)*	*I am known*

Nunc	**autem**	**manet,**	**fides,**	**spes,**	**caritas,**	**tria haec.**
Now	*however*	*remains*	*faith*	*hope*	*charity(love)*	*three these*

Maior	**autem**	**his**	**est**	**caritas.**
Greatest	*however*	*of these*	*is*	*love.*

Sayings. Translate.

1. Sign of the cross ____Signum Crucis____
2. Even one hair has a shadow. ____Etiam capillus unus habet umbram____
3. O excellent protector of sheep, the wolf! _____
   ____O praeclarum custodem ovium lupum____
4. Tibi gratias ago. ____Thank you.____

Grammar

1. Nouns whose genitive singular ends in **ei** belong to the ____fifth____ declension.
2. Most nouns of the fifth declension are ____feminine____ in gender.
   Two exceptions are ____dies____ and ____meridies____.
3. On blank paper, decline: (a) **spes**   (b) **dies bonus**   (c) **facies nova**

Drill A. Give the accusative singular and plural. [All 5th declension]

1. dies	____diem____	____dies____
2. spes	____spem____	____spes____
3. res	____rem____	____res____
4. facie	____faciem____	____facies____

Drill B. Translate. [nouns all 5th declension]

1. in longam aciem	into the long battle line	[acc sg]
2. sancta fides	holy faith	[nom sg]
3. per spem	through hope	[acc sg]
4. sine multis rebus	without many things	[abl pl]
5. ab acie	from the battle line	[abl sg]
6. post meridiem (P.M.)	after midday	[acc sg]
7. bonarum rerum	of good things	[gen pl]
8. multis bonis diebus	to, for; by, with, from many good days	[dat, abl pl]

WORD STUDY

Fifth declension words usually end in *es* in the nominative. The genitive singular ending is *ei*. Students will have some difficulty with these words because of the double vowel and the fact that the stem may end in an *i*. The stem of *dies* is *di*, the stem of *acies* is *aci*, the stem of *res* is *r*. Fifth declension words are feminine unless otherwise noted.

Ab extra:

Carpe diem, Seize the day.
Per diem, per day.

The battle cry of the Protestant reformation was *sola fide*, by faith alone (in the ablative case). The three Christian virtues are:
   fides, spes and *caritas*.

Derivatives

Derivatives

dies	*dial*	spes	*despair*
	diary		*desperado*
fides	*fidelity*	meridies	*meridian*
	infidel		
		facies	*facial*
res	*real*		*facade*
	republic		

Lesson Plan XXIV

Drill C. Translate.   [nouns all 5th declension]

1. to/for many good things _____
   multis et bonis rebus

2. (by) faith alone ____ sola fide ____

3. of faces ____ facierum ____

4. without hope ____ sine spe ____

5. without days ____ sine diebus ____

6. without faith ____ sine fide ____

7. your face ____ facies tua ____

8. of new things ____ rerum novarum ____

Exercises A. Translate.

1. Deus res bonas et multas parat. _____
   God prepares many good things.

2. Christiani fidem et spem habent. _____
   Christians have faith and hope.

3. Miles in acie longa pugnabat. _____
   The soldier was fighting in the long battle line.

4. Puella faciem novam habet. _____
   The girl has a new face.

Exercise B. Translate.

1. My face warns the student. ____ Facies mea discipulum monet. ____

2. The cavalry is coming into the battle line. _____
   Equitatus in aciem venit.

3. God gives hope. ____ Deus spem dat. ____

4. The days are long. ____ Dies sunt longi. ____

Derivatives. Use each derivative in a sentence.

1. fidelity _____

2. facial _____

3. despair _____

4. meridian _____

Lesson Plan XXV

SAYING

Happiness is closely allied to gratitude. *Deo gratias* for another year of Latin!

WORD STUDY

Students should recognize these words as first and second declension adjectives. *Christianus* and *Romanus* can be both nouns and adjectives as they are in English.

Related Latin words/sayings:
alma *mater,*
veritas,
O *prae*clarum *custodem ovium lupum.* Laeti *triumphantes* (Adeste Fidelis*)*.

Latin Saying

Deo gratias

Thanks be to God

Vocabulary

1.	clarus, a, um	*clear, bright, famous*
2.	cupidus, a, um	*eager, desirous*
3.	laetus, a, um	*glad, joyful, happy*
4.	Christianus, a, um	*Christian*
5.	Romanus, a, um	*Roman*
6.	albus, a, um	*white*
7.	alienus, a, um	*unfavorable, foreign*
8.	almus, a , um	*nurturing, kindly*
9.	verus, a, um	*true*
10.	beatus, a, um	*blessed*

Grammar

More practice in using first and second declension adjectives modifying nouns in other declensions.

Sayings. Translate.

1. Day of wrath _____ Dies Irae _____
2. O excellent protector of sheep, the wolf! _____
   _____ O praeclarum custodem ovium lupum. _____
3. O the times, O the customs _____ O tempora, O mores. _____
4. nurturing mother _____ Alma mater _____

Drill A. Translate.

1. clarus vir _____ famous man _____ [2nd decl. masc.]
2. clara femina _____ famous woman _____ [1st decl. fem.]
3. laeti viri _____ happy men _____ [2nd decl. masc.]
4. laetae feminae _____ happy women _____ [1st decl. fem.]
5. agnus albus _____ white lamb _____ [2nd decl. masc.]
6. alienus hostis _____ foreign enemy _____ [3rd decl. masc.]
7. almi amici _____ nurturing friends _____ [2nd decl. masc.]
8. vera fides _____ true faith _____ [5th decl. fem.]
9. Beata Virgo Maria _____ Blessed Virgin Mary _____ [*]
10. vicus Romanus _____ Roman village _____ [2nd decl.]
11. laetus poeta _____ happy poet _____ [1st decl. masc.]
12. virtutes Christianae _____ Christian virtues _____ [3rd decl. fem.]

Drill B. Translate.

1. foreign tribe _____ gens aliena _____ [3rd decl. fem.]
2. kindly heart _____ cor almum _____ [3rd decl. neut.]
3. Christian faith _____ fides Christiana _____ [5th decl. fem.]
4. Roman gods _____ dei Romani _____ [2nd decl. masc.]
5. blessed year _____ annus beatus _____ [2nd decl. masc.]
6. true hope _____ spes vera _____ [5th decl. fem.]
7. true heart _____ cor verum _____ [3rd decl. neut.]

DERIVATIVES

clarus
clarity
clearance
clarify
clarinet

cupidus
Cupid
cupidity

albus
albino

alienus
alien
alienate

verus
verily
verify
verdict

beatus
beatitude

Lesson Plan XXV

8. nurturing faith	fides alma	[5th decl. fem.]
9. white snow	nix alba	[3rd decl. fem.]
10. white sheep (pl.)	oves albae	[3rd decl. fem.]
11. foreign guard	custos alienus	[3rd decl. masc.]
12. eager boy	puer cupidus	[2nd decl. masc.]

Exercise A. Translate.

1. Christiani Veram Fidem habent. Christians have the True Faith.

2. Quid Christianae virtutes sunt? Christianae virtutes sunt Fides, Spes, et Caritas.
   What are the Christian virtues? The Christian virtues are Faith, Hope and Charity.

3. Miles cor cupidum habet. The soldier has an eager heart.

4. Poetae carmen laetum amant. The poets love a happy song.

Exercise B. Translate.

1. Christians will be blessed and happy with Jesus in heaven.
   Christiani cum Jesu in Caelo beati et laeti erunt.

2. The journey was long, but happy.
   Iter longum erat, sed laetum.

3. Roman wars are famous. Bella Romana sunt clara.

4. The Romans were staying with foreign tribes.
   Romani cum gentibus alienis manebant.

Derivatives. Use each derivative in a sentence.

1. Cupid _____

2. albino _____

3. verify _____

4. alien _____

5. clarify _____

Review Lesson E

Grammar Forms

Third declension
neuter

carmen, carminis
cor, cordis,
flumen, fluminis
iter, itineris
jus, juris
mare, maris
opus, operis
os, oris
rus, ruris
ver, veris
vulnus, vulneris

masculine

fons, fontis
sal, salis

Sayings

O Tempora, O mores
Dies Irae
Deo gratias
Etiam capillus unus habet umbram
O praeclarum custodem ovium lupum

Fourth declension

adventus, us
equitatus, us
exercitus, us
fructus, us
impetus, us
lacus, us
portus, us
senatus, us
spiritus, us
usus, us

Other words

autem
diu
etiam
itaque
tatim
tum
undique

Fifth declension

acies, aciei
dies, diei, *m.*
facies, faciei
fides, fidei
meridies, ei, *m.*
res, rei
spes, spei

Adjectives

albus, a, um
alienus, a, um
almus, a, um
beatus, a, um
Christianus, a, um
clarus, a, um
cupidus, a, um
laetus, a, um
Romanus, a, um
verus, a, um

Third Declension
neuter forms

S.	Pl.
flumen	flumina
fluminis	fluminum
flumini	fluminibus
flumen	flumina
flumine	fluminibus

Third Declension
neuter case endings

S.	Pl.
—	a
is	um
i	ibus
—	a
e	ibus

Fourth Declension
forms and case endings

S.	Pl.
port-us	port-us
port-us	port-uum
port-ui	port-ibus
port-um	port-us
port-u	port-ibus

Fifth Declension
forms and case endings

S.	Pl.
r-es	r-es
r-ei	r-erum
r-ei	r-ebus
r-em	r-es
r-e	r-ebus

Assignment

Assign all CALL CARDS for words in this review lesson.

Assign the *Pater Noster* again for students to translate. They know most all of the words and can now identify the cases of many of the words and what part of the sentence they are. Try some other memorized passages or songs for classroom translation.

Drill A. Give the correct form for each noun and translate.

		case/number	form		translation
1.	flumen	dat. Pl.	fluminibus	[3rd decl.]	to, for the rivers
2.	fides	abl. S.	fide	[5th decl.]	by, with, from faith
3.	spiritus	gen. Pl.	spirituum	[2nd decl.]	of the spirits
4.	jus	acc. Pl.	jura	[3rd decl.]	rights
5.	ver	nom. Pl.	vera	[3rd decl.]	springs
6.	lacus	abl. Pl.	lacibus	[4th decl.]	by, with, from the lakes
7.	usus	gen. S.	usus	[4th decl.]	of the use
8.	acies	dat. S.	aciei	[5th decl.]	to, for the battle line
9.	os	acc. S.	os	[3rd decl.]	mouth
10.	sal	dat. S.	sali	[3rd decl.]	to, for the salt

READING # 5
Christiani et Romani

Romani Christianos diu non amabant. Christiani Christum et Deum et Spiritum Sanctum adorabant. Christiani carmina in ecclesia canebant. Christiani in ecclesia panem edebant et vinum bibebant. Christiani veritatem credebant et docebant. Christiani fidem in Christo non in Caesare ponebant. Christiani Caesarem non adorabant.

Romani Christianos puniebant. Erat magna ignis in Roma. Nero, imperator Romanus, Christianos appellabat. "Habetis culpam," inquit[1]. Christiani autem Neronem[2] non timebant quod in Christo fidem ponebant. Nero in Colliseum Christianos jubebat. Leones[3] in Colliseum veniebant. Christiani autem leones non timebant. Christiani orabant et in carminibus Christum laudabant. Christiani pro[4] Christo vitas dabant. Christiani erant laeti et beati. Christiani nunc in Caelo sunt. Laudasne[5] Christianos aut[6] Romanos?

_____

[1] he said
[2] acc. of Nero
[3] nom. pl. of leo
[4] for
[5] ne at end of first word indicates a question
[6] or

Reading #5

For a long time the Romans were not liking (did not like) the Christians. The Christians were adoring (worshipping) Christ, God, and the Holy Spirit. Christians were singing songs in church. Christians were eating bread and drinking wine in church. Christians were teaching and believing the truth. Christians were placing faith in Christ, not in Caesar. Christians were not worshipping (adoring) Caesar.

The Romans were punishing the Christians. There was a great fire in Rome (A great fire was in Rome). Nero, the Roman emperor, addressed the Christians. You have guilt (are guilty), he said. However, the Christians were not fearing Nero because they were placing faith in Christ. Nero was ordering the Christians to the Colosseum. Lions were coming into the Colosseum. However, the Christians were not fearing the lions. The Christians were praying and praising Christ in songs. Christians were giving their lives for Christ. The Christians were happy and blessed and now are in Heaven. Do you praise the Christians or the Romans?

Congratulations on Completing Latina Christiana II
You may request a certificate of accomplishment from the Christian Latin Society at
www.MemoriaPress.com/CLSA

Tests and Keys

Latin II Test I
Lessons 1-5

nomen _____

datum _____

A. Grammar

1. List all five Latin cases.

2. The direct object is always in the _____ case.

3. Fill in these boxes with the usual word order of a Latin sentence.

   [ ] [ ] [ ]

4. Give the nominative and genitive singular endings for each declension.

	First Declension	Second Declension	Third Declension
nominative	_____	_____	_____
genitive	_____	_____	_____

5. Give all three English meanings for *voco* in the present tense.

voco	_____	_____	_____
vocas	_____	_____	_____
vocat	_____	_____	_____
vocamus	_____	_____	_____
vocatis	_____	_____	_____
vocant	_____	_____	_____

B. Sayings. Translate

1. The mother of Italy - Rome _____

2. Ever higher! _____

3. Lamb of God who takes away the sins of the world.

   _____

4. The Roman Peace _____

C. *Forms.* Give the correct forms for each noun.

	Nom. Pl.	Acc. S.	Acc. Pl.
1. gaudium	_____	_____	_____
2. corona	_____	_____	_____
3. locus	_____	_____	_____
4. signum	_____	_____	_____
5. nuntius	_____	_____	_____
6. femina	_____	_____	_____

D. *Forms.* Give the correct form of each verb.

1. They are walking _____ 2. He does work _____

3. I was praying _____ 4. We will move _____

F. *Translation*

1. Roma magnam gloriam amat. _____

2. Deus multa praemia dabit. _____

3. Rex gladios occupabat. _____

4. The people fear the Lord. _____

G. *Vocabulary.* Give the nominative and genitive for nouns.

1. sister _____ 2. ship _____

3. death _____ 4. fire _____

5. dinner _____ 6. bear _____

7. eye _____ 8. sin, mistake _____

9. first _____ 10. against _____

11. often _____ 12. bad _____

Latin II Test II
Lessons 6-10

_____   _____
nomen   datum

A. *Grammar*

   1. The genitive singular is always used to (a) _____

   (b) _____

   2. Three 1st declension nouns that are masculine are : _____

   _____

   3. Give the correct case or cases for the following:

      a. subject   _____

      b. direct object   _____

      c. objects of prepositions _____

   4. Define

      a. subject   _____

      b. direct object   _____

      c. preposition   _____

B. *Vocabulary. Give nominative form and genitive singular ending (or form) for nouns.*

1. door, entrance _____
2. commandment _____
3. altar _____
4. town, village _____
5. across _____
6. without _____
7. time, period, age _____
8. shadow _____
9. enthusiasm, learning _____
10. through _____

11. harp _____
12. farmhouse _____
13. book _____
14. a Gaul _____
15. around, about _____
16. danger, peril _____
17. gate, door _____
18. knowledge _____
19. beginning _____
20. shield _____

C. *Sayings. Translate.*

1. The master has spoken _____

2. Natura non facit saltum _____

3. Retro Satana! _____

4. Hannibal at the gates! _____

5. Repetition is the mother of learning _____

D. *Forms: Decline puer and liber*

E. *Translate*

1. The lamb does not love the wolf.

2. Discipuli libros multos amant.

3. Farmers and poets live in the village.

4. Marcus in casam ambulabat.

Latin II Test III
Lessons 11-15

nomen _____   datum _____

A. *Grammar*

1. Give the endings for the regular principal parts:

    1st conjugation verbs _____

    2nd conjugation verbs _____

2. Give the principal parts for these verbs. The principal parts are irregular.

    a. pono _____

    b. do _____

    c. sto _____

    d. mitto _____

3. Give the principal parts for these verbs. The principal parts are regular.

    a. moneo _____

    b. voco _____

    c. valeo _____

    d. tempto _____

4. Conjugate *sum* in three tenses with English meanings.

B. Forms. Conjugate rego in the present and imperfect tenses.

C. Sayings.

1. I sing of arms and a man. _____

2. Let the buyer beware. _____

3. To err is human. _____

4. I believe in one God. _____

D. Vocabulary. Give the Latin verb with its 2nd principal part.

1. do, drive, act, treat _____ 7. drink _____

2. seek, beg _____ 8. believe _____

3. answer, reply _____ 9. say, tell _____

4. greet _____ 10. laugh _____

5. rule _____ 11. lead, guide _____

6. remain, stay _____ 12. eat _____

E. Translate

1. Pueri et puellae in agro currunt.

2. Girls are warning the boys.

3. Angeli cum citharis et tubis canunt.

4. A book was on the table.

Latin II Test IV
Lessons 16-20

_____   _____
nomen   datum

A. Grammar

1. Give the endings for the regular principal parts.

   a. 1st conjugation _____

   b. 2nd conjugation _____

   c. 4th conjugation _____

2. a. Give the principal parts of *audio.*

   _____

   b. On the back conjugate **audio** with meanings in the present and imperfect tenses.

3. Give the endings for:

                         nominative singular   *genitive singular*

   a. 1st declension _____   _____

   b. 2nd declension _____   _____

   c. 3rd declension _____   _____

4. Decline **lex** and **pars.**

B. *Gender. Give the gender of these nouns and the rule.*

noun	gender	rule
1. lectio, lectionis	_____	_____
2. pastor, pastoris	_____	_____
3. voluntas, voluntatis	_____	_____
4. clamor, clamoris	_____	_____

C. *Sayings.*

1. Carthage must be destroyed. _____

2. I am a citizen of Rome. _____

3. Non oratorem, non senatorem, sed piscatorem.

   _____

4. Hail Caesar, we who are about to die salute you.

   _____

D. *Vocabulary. Give nominative and genitive forms for nouns.*

1. tomorrow _____   11. nothing _____

2. custom _____   12. yesterday_____

3. foot _____   13. love, charity _____

4. tree _____   14. tooth _____

5. bird _____   15. snow _____

6. sheep _____   16. world, orbit, circle _____

7. seat,abode _____   17. freedom, liberty _____

8. suffering _____   18. temptation_____

9. bread _____   19. guard _____

10.because _____   20. who? _____

E. *Translate*

1. A girl is opening the door. _____

2. The leaders and senators praise liberty. _____

3. Lucia panem in mensa ponit. _____

4. Ubi est agnus? _____

Latin II Test V
Lessons 21-25

_____

nomen

datum
_____

A. Grammar

1. Give the nominative and genitive singular endings for each declension.

	Third Declension	Fourth Declension	Fifth Declension
nominative	_____	_____	_____
genitive	_____	_____	_____

2. In Latin, neuter nouns in any declension, singular or plural, always have the same endings in what two cases?
_____

3. Decline (a) flumen   (b) portus   (c) res

B. Vocabulary. Write words with endings given in vocabulary lists. Give gender for ex. cr.

1. heart _____
2. song _____
3. on all sides _____
4. lake, pit _____
5. midday _____
6. true _____
7. glad, happy _____
8. face _____
9. mouth _____
10. journey _____

11. sea _____
12. fountain _____
13. at once, immediately _____
14. attack _____
15. battle line _____
16. blessed _____
17. white _____
18. army _____
19. however _____
20. work, deed _____

C. Sayings

1. Day of Wrath _____

2. O the times, O the customs _____

3. Deo gratias _____

4. O excellent protector of sheep, the wolf.

_____

5. Etiam capillus unus habet umbram.

_____

D. Translate.

1. Multi oves et agni in rure sunt.

_____

2. Miles cor cupidum habet.

_____

3. Poets love a happy song.

_____

Test Key

Test I

A. Grammar
1. nominative, genitive, dative, accusative, ablative
2. accusative
3. subject   direct object   verb
4.   a   us, um   varies (—)
      ae   i   is

5. I call, do call, am calling
   you call, do call, are calling
   he, she, it calls, does call, is calling
   we call, do call, are calling
   you call, do call, are calling
   they call, do call, are calling

B. Sayings
1. Mater Italiae - Roma
2. Excelsior!
3. Agnus Dei qui tollis peccata mundi.
4. Pax Romana

C. Forms
1. gaudia, gaudium, gaudia
2. coronae, coronam, coronas
3. loci, locum, locos
4. signa, signum, signa
5. nuntii, nuntium, nuntios
6. feminae, feminam, feminas

D. Forms
1. ambulant
2. laborat
3. orabam
4. movebimus

E. Translation
1. Rome loves great glory.
2. God will give many rewards.
3. The king was seizing the swords.
4. Populus Dominum timet.

F. Vocabulary
1. soror, sororis
2. navis, navis
3. mors, mortis
4. ignis, ignis
5. cena, cenae
6. ursa, ursae
7. oculus, oculi
8. peccatum, peccati
9. primus, a, um
10. contra
11. saepe
12. malus, a, um

Test II

A. Grammar
1. (a) identify the declension, (b) find the stem.
2. nauta, poeta, agricola
3. a. nominative
   b. accusative
   c. accusative and ablative
4. a. The subject is the thing or person that performs the action of the verb.
   b. The direct object is the thing or person that receives the action of the verb.
   c. A preposition is a word that shows the relationship between a noun (or pronoun) and a other word in the sentence.

B. Vocabulary
1. janua, ae
2. mandatum, i
3. ara, ae
4. vicus, i
5. trans
6. sine
7. saeculum, i
8. umbra, ae
9. studium i
10. per
11. cithara, ae
12. villa, ae
13. liber, libri
14. Gallus, i
15. circum
16. periculum, i
17. porta, ae
18. scientia, ae
19. principium, i
20. scutum, i

C. Sayings
1. Magister dixit.
2. Nature does not make leaps.
3. Get thee behind me Satan.
4. Hannibal ad portas!
5. Repetitio mater studiorum.

D. Forms

puer	pueri	liber	libri
pueri	puerorum	libri	librorum
puero	pueris	libro	libris
puerum	pueros	librum	libros
puero	pueris	libro	libris

E. Translate
1. Agnus lupum non amat.
2. Students love many books.
3. Agricolae et poetae in vico habitant.
4. Mark was walking into the cottage.

Test III

A. Grammar

1. o, are, avi, atus
   eo, ére, ui, itus
2. a. pono, ponere, posui, positus
   b. do, dare, dedi, datus
   c. sto, stare, steti, status
   d. mitto, mittere, misi, missus
3. a. moneo, monére, monui, monitus
   b. voco, vocare, vocavi, vocatus
   c. valeo, valére, valui, valitus
   d. tempto, temptare, temptavi, temptatus

4.

sum	*I am*	sumus	*we are*
es	*you are*	estis	*you are*
est	*he, she, it is*	sunt	*they are*
eram	*I was*	erámus	*we were*
eras	*you were*	erátis	*you were*
erat	*he, she, it was*	erant	*they were*
ero	*I will be*	érimus	*we will be*
eris	*you will be*	éritis	*you will be*
erit	*he, she, it will be*	erunt	*they will be*

B. Forms

rego	regimus	regebam	regebamus
regis	regitis	regebas	regebatis
regit	regunt	regebat	regebant

C. Sayings

1. Arma virumque cano.
2. caveat emptor
3. Errare est humanum.
4. Credo in unum Deum.

D. Vocabulary

1. ago, agere
2. peto, petere
3. respondeo, respondére
4. saluto, salutare
5. rego, regere
6. maneo, manére
7. bibo, bibere
8. credo, credere
9. dico, dicere
10. rideo, ridére
11. duco, ducere
12. edo, edere

E. Translate

1. Boys and girls are running in the field.
2. Puellae pueros monent.
3. Angels are singing with harps and trumpets.
4. Liber in mensa erat.

Test IV

A. Grammar

1. a. o, are, avi, atus
   b. eo, ére, ui, itus
   c. io, ire, ivi, itus

2. a. audio, audire, audivi, auditus

   b.

audio	*I hear*	audimus	*we hear*
audis	*you hear*	auditis	*you hear*
audit	*he, she, it hears*	audiunt	*they hear*
audiebam	*I was hearing*	audiebamus	*we were hearing*
audiebas	*you were hearing*	audiebatis	*you were hearing*
audiebat	*he, she, it was hearing*	audiebant	*they were hearing*

3. a. a   ae
   b. us, um, er, ir   i
   c. varies   is

4.

lex	leges	pars	partes
legis	legum	partis	partium
legi	legibus	parti	partibus
legem	leges	partem	partes
lege	legibus	parte	partibus

B. Gender
   1. feminine   feminine endings rule (tio, tionis)
   2. masculine   natural gender, shepherds were all men
   3. feminine   feminine endings rule, (tas, tatis)
   4. masculine   masculine endings rule (or, oris)

C. Sayings
   1. Delenda est Carthago
   2. Romanus civis sum
   3. Not an orator, not a senator, but a fisherman
   4. Ave Caesar, morituri te salutamus

D. Vocabulary
   1. cras
   2. mos, moris
   3. pes, pedis
   4. arbor, arboris
   5. avis, avis
   6. ovis, ovis
   7. sedes, sedis
   8. passio, passionis
   9. panis, panis
   10. quod
   11. nihil
   12. heri
   13. caritas, caritatis
   14. dens, dentis
   15. nix, nivis
   16. orbis, orbis
   17. libertas, libertatis
   18. tentatio, tentationis
   19. custos, custodis
   20. quis

E. Translate
   1. Puella januam aperit.
   2. Duces et senatores libertatem laudant.
   3. Lucy is putting bread on the table.
   4. Where is the lamb?

Test Key

Test V

A. Grammar

1.

varies	us	es
is	us	ei

2. nominative and accusative

3.

flumen	flumina	portus	portus	res	res
fluminis	fluminum	portus	portuum	rei	rerum
flumini	fluminibus	portui	portibus	rei	rebus
flumen	flumina	portum	portus	rem	res
flumine	fluminibus	portu	portibus	re	rebus

B. Vocabulary

1. cor, cordis, *n.*
2. carmen, carminis, *n.*
3. undique
4. lacus, us, *m.*
5. meridies, ei, *m.*
6. verus, a, um
7. laetus, a, um
8. facies, ei, *f.*
9. os, oris, *n.*
10. iter, itineris, *n.*
11. mare, maris, *n.*
12. fons, fontis, *n.*
13. statim
14. impetus, us, *m.*
15. acies, ei, *f.*
16. beatus, a, um
17. albus, a, um
18. exercitus, us, *m.*
19. autem
20. opus, operis, *n*

C. Sayings

1. Dies Irae
2. O tempora, O mores
3. Thanks be to God
4. O praeclarum custodem ovium lupum
5. Even one hair has a shadow

D. Translate

1. Many sheep and lambs are in the countryside.
2. The soldier has an eager heart.
3. Poetae carmen laetum amant.

Lesson 1 Quiz

Latin Saying

Ora et Labora
Labor omnia vincit.

_____

_____

Vocabulary

1. navigo
2. specto
3. terreo
4. paro
5. jubeo
6. doceo

_____

_____

_____

_____

_____

_____

Grammar Forms

voco, future tense:

_____ _____

_____ _____

_____ _____

video, present tense:

_____ _____

_____ _____

_____ _____

sedeo, imperfect tense:

_____ _____

_____ _____

_____ _____

judico, present tense:

_____ _____

_____ _____

_____ _____

Lesson 2 Quiz

Latin Saying

Senatus Populusque Romanus   _____

stupor mundi   _____

Vocabulary

1. silva   _____
2. mora   _____
3. culpa   _____
4. nauta   _____
5. injuria   _____
6. cena   _____

Grammar Forms

List the cases and the first declension endings:

_____

_____

_____

_____

_____

Second person pronouns, singular and plural:

_____   _____

_____   _____

_____   _____

_____   _____

_____   _____

Lesson 3 Quiz

Latin Saying

Novus ordo seclorum
Veni, vidi, vici

_____

_____

Vocabulary

1. locus
2. tergum
3. hortus
4. ludus
5. auxilium
6. gaudium

_____

_____

_____

_____

_____

_____

Grammar Forms

Decline gladius and verbum:

_____ _____   _____ _____

_____ _____   _____ _____

_____ _____   _____ _____

_____ _____   _____ _____

_____ _____   _____ _____

Lesson 4 Quiz

Latin Saying

Vox Populi, Vox Dei   _____

Signum crucis   _____

Vocabulary

1. urbs   _____
2. nox   _____
3. veritas   _____
4. miles   _____
5. collis   _____
6. pons   _____

Grammar Forms

Give the genitive singular:

gens   _____
vox   _____
virtus   _____
flumen   _____
canis   _____

Count from one through ten:

_____

Lesson 5 Quiz

Vocabulary

1. tutus, a, um
2. plenus, a, um
3. proximus, a, um
4. solus, a, um
5. aeternus, a, um
6. certus, a, um

_____
_____
_____
_____
_____
_____

Grammar Forms

Decline magnus in the plural:

_____ _____ _____

_____ _____ _____

_____ _____ _____

_____ _____ _____

_____ _____ _____

Adverbs, Prepositions, Conjunctions

Translate:

clam _____   contra _____

sicut _____   saepe _____

Lesson 6 Quiz

Latin Saying

Retro Satana!   _____

Vocabulary

1. fabula   _____
2. sella   _____
3. umbra   _____
4. villa   _____
5. porta   _____

Grammar Forms

Decline porta:

_____   _____

_____   _____

_____   _____

_____   _____

_____   _____

Lesson 7 Quiz

Latin Saying

Natura non facit saltum   _____

Vocabulary

1. culina
2. ara
3. scientia
4. casa
5. epistula

_____
_____
_____
_____
_____

Grammar Forms

Identify case and number; define:

januas   _____
tabellarum _____
poetis   _____
scientiae   _____
agricolam   _____

Give the accusative singular and plural:

natura bona _____
poeta malus _____

Lesson 8 Quiz

Latin Saying

Magister dixit.   _____

Vocabulary

1. vicus   _____
2. lupus   _____
3. ager   _____
4. Gallus   _____
5. liber, libri   _____

Grammar Forms

Decline magister:

_____   _____

_____   _____

_____   _____

_____   _____

_____   _____

Lesson 9 Quiz

Latin Saying

Repetitio mater studiorum   _____

Vocabulary

1. mandatum   _____
2. vir   _____
3. studium   _____
4. scutum   _____
5. periculum   _____

Grammar Forms

Decline vir:

_____   _____

_____   _____

_____   _____

_____   _____

Lesson 10 Quiz

Latin Saying

Hannibal ad portas!   _____

Vocabulary

1. de   _____
2. a, ab   _____
3. sine   _____
4. per   _____
5. trans   _____

Grammar Forms

Give the correct form of oppidum and casa:

circum   _____   _____

sine   _____   _____

per   _____   _____

de   _____   _____

ad   _____   _____

Lesson 11 Quiz

Grammar Forms

Conjugate sum in the present, imperfect and future tenses:

_____   _____

_____   _____

_____   _____

_____   _____

_____   _____

_____   _____

_____   _____

_____   _____

Translate:

A horse is in the garden.   _____

The reward of knowledge will be great.   _____

A small army was near the gates of the city. _____

Lesson 12 Quiz

Latin Saying

Errare est humanum   _____

Vocabulary

1. saluto   _____
2. sto   _____
3. exspecto   _____
4. do   _____
5. nato   _____

Grammar Forms

Conjugate ero in the imperfect tense and do in the future tense:

_____   _____

_____   _____

_____   _____

_____   _____

_____   _____

Lesson 13 Quiz

Latin Saying

Caveat emptor   _____

Vocabulary

1. rideo   _____
2. maneo   _____
3. augeo   _____
4. moneo   _____
5. respondeo   _____

Grammar Forms

Conjugate teneo in the present tense and fleo in the imperfect tense:

_____   _____

_____   _____

_____   _____

_____   _____

_____   _____

_____   _____

Lesson 14 Quiz

Latin Saying

Credo in unum Deum.   _____

Vocabulary

1. trado   _____
2. cado   _____
3. curro   _____
4. bibo   _____
5. pono   _____

Grammar Forms

Conjugate credo and vivo in the present tense:

_____   _____

_____   _____

_____   _____

_____   _____

_____   _____

_____   _____

Lesson 15 Quiz

Latin Saying

Arma virumque cano   _____

Vocabulary

1. claudo   _____
2. mitto   _____
3. edo   _____
4. tollo   _____
5. peto   _____

Grammar Forms

Conjugate cano and dico in the imperfect tense:

_____   _____

_____   _____

_____   _____

_____   _____

_____   _____

Nomen _____   **Datum** _____

Lesson 16 Quiz

Latin Saying

Ave Caesar, morituri te salutamus   _____

Vocabulary

1. finio   _____
2. aperio   _____
3. scio   _____
4. sentio   _____
5. venio   _____

Grammar Forms

Conjugate dormio and munio in the present tense:

_____   _____

_____   _____

_____   _____

_____   _____

_____   _____

_____   _____

Lesson 17 Quiz

Latin Saying

Hodie Christus natus est.   _____

Vocabulary

1. cur   _____
2. ubi   _____
3. heri   _____
4. cras   _____
5. hodie   _____

Grammar Forms

Conjugate punio and sentio in the imperfect tense:

_____   _____

_____   _____

_____   _____

_____   _____

_____   _____

_____   _____

Lesson 18 Quiz

Latin Saying

Non oratorem, non senatorem,
sed piscatorem.

_____

Vocabulary

1. pastor, pastoris
2. clamor, clamoris
3. lectio, lectionis
4. mos, moris
5. timor, timoris

_____
_____
_____
_____
_____

Grammar Forms

Decline mos:

_____   _____

_____   _____

_____   _____

_____   _____

Lesson 19 Quiz

Latin Saying

Delenda est Carthago.   _____

Vocabulary

1. pes, pedis   _____
2. panis, panis   _____
3. sol, solis   _____
4. arbor, arboris   _____
5. dux, ducis   _____

Grammar Forms

Decline dux:

_____   _____

_____   _____

_____   _____

_____   _____

_____   _____

Lesson 20 Quiz

Latin Saying

Romanus civis sum.

_____

Vocabulary

1. dens, dentis
2. avis, avis
3. ars, artis
4. sedes, sedis
5. orbis, orbis

_____
_____
_____
_____
_____

Grammar Forms

Decline civis:

_____   _____

_____   _____

_____   _____

_____   _____

_____   _____

Lesson 21 Quiz

Latin Saying

O tempora, O mores!   _____

Vocabulary

1. mare, maris   _____
2. iter, itineris   _____
3. cor, cordis   _____
4. flumen, fluminis   _____
5. opus, operis   _____

Grammar Forms

Decline mare:

_____   _____

_____   _____

_____   _____

_____   _____

_____   _____

Lesson 22 Quiz

Latin Saying

Etiam capillus unus habet umbram.   _____

Vocabulary

1. itaque   _____
2. tum   _____
3. statim   _____
4. diu   _____
5. autem   _____

Grammar Forms

Decline fons:

_____   _____

_____   _____

_____   _____

_____   _____

Lesson 23 Quiz

Latin Saying

O praeclarum custodem ovium lupum.   _____

Vocabulary

1. spiritus, us   _____
2. usus, us   _____
3. portus, us   _____
4. fructus, us   _____
5. exercitus, us   _____

Grammar Forms

Decline lacus:

_____   _____

_____   _____

_____   _____

_____   _____

Lesson 24 Quiz

Latin Saying

Dies Irae

_____

Vocabulary

1. fides, fidei
2. spes, spei
3. facies, faciei
4. meridies, meridiei
5. res, rei

_____
_____
_____
_____
_____

Grammar Forms

Decline dies:

_____   _____

_____   _____

_____   _____

_____   _____

_____   _____

Lesson 25 Quiz

Latin Saying

Deo gratias   _____

Vocabulary

1. albus, a, um   _____
2. laetus, a, um   _____
3. verus, a, um   _____
4. clarus, a, um   _____
5. alienus, a, um   _____

Grammar Forms

Decline mens clara:

_____   _____

_____   _____

_____   _____

_____   _____

_____   _____

ANSWER KEYS TO QUIZ PAGES

Lesson 1.

Latin Saying:	Work and Pray
	Work conquers all.
Vocabulary:	1. I sail
	2. I look at
	3. I frighten
	4. I prepare
	5. I order
	6. I teach
Grammar:	vocabo, vocabis, vocabit, vocabimus, vocabitis, vocabunt
	video, vides, videt, videmus, videtis, vident
	sedebam, sedebas, sedebat, sedebamus, sedebatis, sedebant
	judico, judicas, judicat, judicamus, judicatis, judicant

Lesson 2.

Latin Saying:	The Senate and the People of Rome
	wonder of the world
Vocabulary:	1. forest
	2. delay
	3. fault, crime
	4. sailor
	5. injury
	6. dinner
Grammar:	nominative, genitive, dative, accusative, ablative
	tu, tui, tibi, te, te vos, vestri/vestrum, vobis, vos, vobis

Lesson 3.

Latin Saying:	New order of the ages
	I came, I saw, I conquered.
Vocabulary:	1. place
	2. back
	3. garden
	4. school, game
	5. help
	6. joy
Grammar:	gladius, gladii, gladio, gladium, gladio
	gladii, gladiorum, gladiis, gladios, gladiis
	verbum, verbi, verbo, verbum, verbo
	verba, verborum, verbis, verba, verbis

Quiz Answer Keys

Lesson 4.

Latin Saying:	The voice of the people is the voice of God.
	Sign of the cross
Vocabulary:	1. city
	2. night
	3. truth
	4. soldier
	5. hill
	6. bridge
Grammar:	gentis, vocis, virtutis, fluminis, canis
	unus, duo, tres, quattuor, quinque, sex, septem, octo, novem, decem

Lesson 5.

Vocabulary:	1. safe
	2. full
	3. next, nearest
	4. alone, only
	5. eternal, everlasting
	6. certain, sure
Grammar:	magni, magnorum, magnis, magnos, magnis
	magnae, magnarum, magnis, magnas, magnis
	magna, magnorum, magnis, magna, magnis
Adverbs, etc.:	secretly, as, against, often

Lesson 6.

Latin Saying:	Get thee behind me, Satan!
Vocabulary:	1. story
	2. chair
	3. shadow
	4. farmhouse
	5. gate
Grammar:	porta, portae, portae, portam, porta
	portae, portarum, portis, portas, portis

Lesson 7.

Latin Saying:	Nature does not make jumps.	
Vocabulary:	1. kitchen	
	2. altar	
	3. knowledge	
	4. cottage	
	5. letter	
Grammar:	acc. pl.	doors

gen. pl.	of the tablets
dat., abl. pl	to, for; by, with, from the poets
gen., dat. sing; nom. pl.	knowledge
acc. sing.	farmer
naturam bonam	naturas bonas
poetam malum	poetas malos

Lesson 8.

Latin Saying: The master has spoken.

Vocabulary:
1. village
2. wolf
3. field
4. Gaul
5. book

Grammar: magister, magistri, magistro, magistrum, magistro
magistri, magistrorum, magistris, magistros, magistris

Lesson 9.

Latin Saying: Repetition is the mother of learning.

Vocabulary:
1. command, commandment
2. man
3. enthusiasm, zeal, learning
4. shield
5. danger

Grammar: vir, viri, viro, virum, viro
viri, virorum, viris, viros, viris

Lesson 10.

Latin Saying: Hannibal at the gates!

Vocabulary:
1. from, down from
2. from, away from
3. without
4. through
5. across

Grammar: oppidum, casam
oppido, casa
oppidum, casam
oppido, casa
oppidum, casam

Quiz Answer Keys

Lesson 11.
Grammar: sum, es, est, sumus, estis, sunt
                             eram, eras, erat, eramus, eratis, erant
                             ero, eris, erit, erimus, eritis, erunt
                             Equus est in horto.
                             Sapientiae praemium erit magnum.
                             Exercitus parvus erat urbis ad portas.

Lesson 12.
Latin Saying: To err is human.
Vocabulary: 1. I greet
                             2. I stand
                             3. I wait for
                             4. I give
                             5. I swim
Grammar: errabam, errabas, errabat, errabamus, errabatis, errabant
                             dabo, dabis, dabit, dabimus, dabitis, dabunt

Lesson 13.
Latin Saying: Let the buyer beware.
Vocabulary: 1. I laugh
                             2. I remain, I stay
                             3. I increase
                             4. I warn
                             5. I answer, I reply
Grammar: teneo, tenes, tenet, tenemus, tenetis, tenent
                             felbam, flebas, flebat, flebamus, flebatis, flebant

Lesson 14.
Latin Saying: I believe in one God.
Vocabulary: 1. I hand over
                             2. I fall
                             3. I run
                             4. I drink
                             5. I place
Grammar: credo, credis, credit, credimus, creditis, credunt
                             vivo, vivis, vivit, vivimus, vivitis, vivunt

Lesson 15.

Latin Saying:	I sing of arms and a man.
Vocabulary:	I close
	2. I send
	3. I eat
	4. I raise up, I take away
	5. I seek, I beg
Grammar:	canebam, canebas, canebat, canebamus, canebatis, canebant
	dicebam, dicebas, dicebat, dicebamus, dicebatis, dicebant

Lesson 16.

Latin Saying:	Hail Caesar, we who are about to die salute you.
Vocabulary:	1. I finish
	2. I open
	3. I know
	4. I feel
	5. I come
Grammar:	dormio, dormis, dormit, dormimus, dormitis, dormiunt
	munio, munis, munit, munimus, minitis, muniunt

Lesson 17.

Latin Saying:	Today Christ is born.
Vocabulary:	1. why
	2. where
	3. yesterday
	4. tomorrow
	5. today
Grammar:	puniebam, puniebas, puniebat, puniebamus, puniebatis, puniebant
	sentiebam, sentiebas, sentiebat, sentiebamus, sentiebatis, sentiebant

Lesson 18.
Latin Saying: Not an orator, not a senator, but a fisherman
Vocabulary: 1. shepherd
                  2. shouting, shout
                  3. lesson
                  4. custom
                  5. fear
Grammar: mos, moris, mori, morem, more
                  mores, morum, moribus, mores, moribus

Lesson 19.
Latin Saying: Carthage must be destroyed.
Vocabulary: 1. foot
                  2. bread
                  3. sun
                  4. tree
                  5. leader
Grammar: dux, ducis, duci, ducem, duce
                  duces, ducum, ducibus, duces, ducibus

Lesson 20.
Latin Saying: I am a citizen of Rome.
Vocabulary: 1. tooth
                  2. bird
                  3. art, skill
                  4. seat, abode
                  5. world, orbit, circle
Grammar: civis, civis, civi, civem, cive
                  cives, civium, civibus, cives, civibus

Lesson 21.
Latin Saying: O the times, O the customs!
Vocabulary: 1. sea
                  2. journey
                  3. heart
                  4. river
                  5. work, deed
Grammar: mare, maris, mari, mare, mari
                  maria, marium, maribus, maria, maribus

Lesson 22.
Latin Saying: Even one hair has a shadow.
Vocabulary: 1. therefore
                   2. then, at that time
                   3. at once, immediately
                   4. for a long time
                   5. however
Grammar: fons, fontis, fonti, fontem, fonte
                   fontes, fontium, fontibus, fontes, fontibus

Lesson 23.
Latin Saying: O excellent protector of sheep, the wolf.
Vocabulary: 1. spirit
                   2. use, experience
                   3. harbor
                   4. fruit, profit, enjoyment
                   5. army
Grammar: lacus, lacus, lacui, lacum, lacu
                   lacus, lacuum, lacibus, lacus, lacibus

Lesson 24.
Latin Saying: Day of Wrath
Vocabulary: 1. faith, loyalty
                   2. hope
                   3. face
                   4. midday, noon
                   5. thing
Grammar: dies, diei, diei, diem, die
                   dies, dierum, diebus, dies, diebus

Lesson 25.
Latin Saying: Thanks be to God.
Vocabulary: 1. white
                   2. glad, joyful, happy
                   3. true
                   4. clear, bright, famous
                   5. unfavorable, foreign
Grammar: mens clara, mentis clarae, menti clarae, mentem claram, mente clara
                   mentes clarae, mentum clararum, mentibus claris, mentes claras,
                   mentibus claris

History Guide
and Key

History Guide and Key

Questions with an asterisk are not completely answered in Famous Men of Rome.

Chapter 14

1. What were the three wars with Carthage called? The Punic Wars
2. What does the word Punic mean? Punic refers to Roman name for Phoenicia.
3. *How long did it take Rome to conquer and unify most of Italy?
    About 500 years, from 753 B.C. to 264 B.C.
4. What military advantage did Carthage have over Rome? Carthage had a navy.
5. *Contrast the economies of Rome and Carthage.
    Rome was originally based on a farming economy. Carthage was a great commercial city, engaging in trade throughout the Mediterranean world. Romans thought the only honorable work for a man was farming or soldiering. Carthaginians were sailors and traders.
6. *Contrast the religions of Rome and Carthage.
    Rome worshipped the pagan gods similar to those of the Greek religion. Romans were especially devoted to the domestic gods of hearth and home. Carthage received her religion from her motherland, Phoenicia. It was the religion, described in the Bible, as the worship of Baal or Moloch. It involved human sacrifice, especially of infants, on a very large scale and was the most evil religion in the ancient world.
7. What piece of land was the First Punic War fought over? Sicily
8. How did Regulus become a prisoner of Carthage?
    Regulus took a Roman army to northern Africa to defeat Carthage, but lost the battle and was captured.
9. What two things did Regulus value over his own life?
    Regulus valued his word, and the welfare and honor of Rome.

Chapter 15

1. Where did the Second Punic War begin? Spain
2. How did Scipio make the Spaniards allies of Rome? By acts of kindness
3. What great obstacle did Hannibal cross to reach Italy? The Alps
4. *Why did Hannibal always defeat the Roman generals in battles? What special weapon did he have?
    Hannibal was one of the greatest generals in history; he had brilliant strategy and used the topography of the land to his advantage. Hannibal had elephants.
5. What is a Fabian policy and how did it get its name? A fabian policy is one of delay, avoiding a direct confrontation, attempting to defeat the enemy by wearing him down rather than winning a pitched battle. It got its name from the Roman general Fabius who used this tactic rather than meeting Hannibal in a direct battle, which he knew he could not win.
6. Where was Hannibal's greatest victory? At the battle of Cannae, the Romans lost 70,000 men.
7. Why did Hannibal go back to Carthage?
    Scipio took an army to north Africa and Hannibal went back to defend Carthage.
8. What offer did Hannibal make to Scipio before the battle of Zama? Hannibal offered to divide the Mediterranean Sea between Rome and Carthage, so that both could be great nations.
9. Who did Hannibal think were the three greatest generals that had ever lived?
    Alexander the Great, Pyrrhus, Hannibal.
10. *Carthage was led by one of the greatest generals in history who invaded Italy and came near to the gates of Rome. Why didn't Hannibal take the city of Rome and why did Carthage ultimately lose the Second Punic War? Hannibal did not have the seige equipment necessary to take a large and well fortified city like Rome. Hannibal received very little support from the Italian people who, he had hoped, would rise up against Rome and follow him as their liberator. The Italian allies of Rome were, for the most part, loyal to her. Carthage foolishly failed to send reinforcements to Hannibal that would have enabled him to complete the conquest of Rome, preferring instead to enjoy its wealth, material comforts, and pleasures of city life. The people of Carthage did not have the spirit of sacrifice and love of country that enabled Rome to always defeat her enemies. The discipline and virtues of Rome defeated the genius and wealth of Carthage.

Chapter 16

1. Why is Cato called Cato the Censor? Describe his personality?
    Cato did the job of censor so well that he was thereafter identified with it and it with him. He brought discipline back to Rome. Cato was serious, disciplined, severe, humorless.

2. How did Cato end every speech in the Senate? *Delenda est Carthago*: Carthage must be destroyed.
3. What unreasonable demand did Rome make of Carthage that caused the Third Punic War?
   Rome asked Carthage to move the city ten miles inland.
4. Rome's struggle with Carthage covered what time period? 264 B.C. - 146 B.C., 118 years

Chapter 17

1. Who was the mother of the Gracchi and what did she call her sons?
   Cornelia, the daughter of Scipio, called her sons, her jewels.
2. How had the patricians been unjust to the plebeians? The patricians had ceased to observe the ancient custom of dividing up the public lands with the plebeians. All of the land went to the nobles who worked it with slaves and the plebeians who had fought in the wars of conquest had no farms to till.
3. What law did Tiberius Gracchus get passed that caused the nobles to hate him?
   He proposed a land distribution law: the nobles would get 500 acres plus 250 acres for each son, and the rest of the public lands would be divided among the plebeians.
4. *Who was elected tribune after Tiberius was killed? His brother, Caius.
5. What falsehood did the nobles spread about both of the Gracchi?
   The nobles said that the Gracchi wanted to be kings.
6. Why did Caius Gracchus ask his slave to kill him?
   In order to prevent war between the nobles and plebeians.

Chapter 18

1. After the Gracchi were both killed, what great man came forward as champion of the plebeians?
   Marius
2. Why were the nobles unable to get rid of Marius?
   They needed him for the defense of Rome because he was such a great general.
3. What three barbarian tribes threatened Rome and where were they from?
   The Cimbri, Teutones, and Ambrones were from the shores of the Baltic Sea in northern Europe.
4. * Contrast the fighting style of the barbarians and the Romans. The barbarians relied upon emotion and physical strength to win battles. The Romans relied upon discipline, organization, and skill. The battle cry and savage appearance of the barbarians is similar to the American Indian preparation for battle.
5. What did the Cimbri ask of Marius and what was his reply? They asked for land and he said "Never mind the Teutones and Ambrones, they have lands already. We have given them some which they will keep forever. We will give you the same".
6. What was the Social War and what general gained fame from it? The Social War was a war between Rome and her socii, allies, in Italy. The Italian tribes and nations had made a great contribution to Rome's struggle with Carthage and now wanted to be rewarded with the benefits of citizenship. Sulla gained great praise because of the Social War and was said to be a better general than Marius.
7. In what war did the Senate appoint Sulla commander, and the tribunes appoint Marius commander?
   The war against Mithridates, king of Pontus.
8. What did Marius tell a solider to tell to the Roman governor of Africa?
   "Go tell your governor that you saw Caius Marius sitting on the ruins of Carthage."
9. How did Marius regain control of Rome and what did he do?
   While Sulla was in the east fighting Mithridates, Cinna raised an army for the plebeian party and asked Marius to come back to Rome. Marius took revenge on the supporters of Sulla, killing many of them. He died two weeks after becoming consul for the seventh time.

Chapter 19

1. Who was aiding the Greeks in their rebellion against Rome? Mithridates, king of Pontus.
2. Why was Athens so difficult to conquer? It was the most strongly fortified city in the ancient world.
3. What weapon did Sulla use to break down the walls of Athens? A battering ram.
4. Who was in control of Rome when Sulla returned from his war against the Greeks?
   The Marian party, Cinna, and Marius the Younger.

History Guide and Key

5. Describe Sulla's "Reign of Terror" and his Triumph?

All of the followers of Marius were hunted out of their hiding places and killed without mercy. Every day a list was made up of those to be found and killed. In the Triumph, Sulla rode in a splendid chariot like a king, followed by a parade of soldiers, slaves, and wagons full of riches captured in the war.

6. What did Sulla do when he tired of being dictator?

He resigned as dictator and retired to his villa in Naples, passing his time in feasting, merriment and study.

Chapter 20

1. What did the "sea rovers" or pirates do and where were they from?

People living on the coasts of Asia Minor built fast ships and raided trading ships and coastal communities.

2. How did Pompey defeat them? Pompey divided the Mediterranean Sea up into 13 districts and sent a fleet of Roman ships into each district to hunt the pirates down and destroy them and their ships.

3. Why was Pompey so popular with the people, even though he was a dictator?

Pompey entertained the people in a new large theater, seating 40,000, with wonderful exhibitions and games. He established a gladiator school. While the people were amused, he ran the government to suit himself.

4. Was Pompey a friend of the Marians or Sulla? Pompey had fought with Sulla against the Marians.

Chapter 21

1. Why was Julius Caesar the greatest Roman of all? Julius Caesar was a great writer, orator, general, politician. A few men in history excel in one or two of these fields; no other man in history excelled in all of them.

2. Who was Caesar's aunt? Caesar's aunt was the wife of Marius.

3. What did Sulla say about Caesar? "In that young man, there is many a Marius."

4. Was Caesar a friend of the nobles or the plebeians? The plebeians.

5. What was Caesar's first important political appointment? Governor of Spain

6. How many men were in a legion? 3000

7. What bird was on the military standard of the legions? eagle

8. *What large area of Europe did Caesar conquer and bring into the Roman Empire? How long did it take him? What is the name of his military journal of this war?

Caesar's campaign in Gaul took 8 years. His military journal is *De Bello Gallico*, About the Gallic War. It is traditionally read in the second year of Latin study in high school.

9. Who was the ruler of Rome when Caesar was ready to return after his conquest of Gaul? Pompey

10. What did Pompey do when Caesar refused to disband his armies, as Pompey had ordered?

Pompey passed a law that Caesar was a public enemy and must be put down.

11. What river on the southern boundary of Gaul did Caesar cross to enter into Italy? Rubicon

12. Where did the armies of Pompey and Caesar meet? In the plain of Pharsalia, in Thessaly, a district of Greece.

13. Where was Pompey killed and by whom?

Pompey was treacherously killed in Egypt by order of Ptolemy, the king.

14. Some of the nobles and senators formed an army which was defeated by Caesar in Asia Minor. What famous dispatch did Caesar send to the Senate after this victory? "Veni, vidi, vici."

15. After Caesar defeated all of his enemies and was made dictator for life, what title showed that he was in command of all of the armies of the Empire? Emperor

16. How was the Julian calendar an improvement over the one it replaced?

He corrected the calendar by adding a day every four years.

17. What warning was given to Caesar by an augur who stopped him on the way to the Forum?

Beware the ides of March. Ides is the 15th of the month.

18. The most highly respected of the conspirators was also a personal friend of Caesar. Who was he?

Brutus

19. How did the assassins of Caesar defend their actions to the people?

They said they had "saved the republic" by keeping Caesar from becoming a king.

20. What famous Roman made an eloquent speech at Caesar's funeral? Mark Antony.

William Shakespeare later dramatized his speech in the play *Julius Caesar.*

History Guide and Key

**These questions are suitable for class discussions, especially for older students.
A variety of opinions may be expressed. Some suggested answers follow.**

*A. How did Caesar increase his popularity with the people? Is vote buying a problem in all democracies and republics?

Caesar, like Pompey, lavished much of his money on the people with entertainments and games. The influence of money on elections is a problem in all republics, as it is in America today.

*B. What does the expression "he has crossed the Rubicon" mean?

It means that a person has taken a fateful step from which there is no turning back. The step has grave consequences. Caesar is reputed to have said at that crossing "The die is cast."

*C. Why did the death of Caesar fail to "save the Republic"? The Roman virtues necessary for self-government had already been destroyed by the wealth and power that had come to Rome through her conquest of other nations. Sulla, Marius, Pompey and Caesar had all been dictators because the Senate no longer had the respect and moral authority necessary to rule the people. Republican government could not be restored to Rome by killing Caesar.

*D. Is it possible for a nation to be a Republic and have an Empire at the same time? Why? Which is better?

A republic is based on self-government; empire is the governing of foreign peoples. There is a fundamental conflict between these two. This is illustrated by the demand of the Italian allies for Roman citizenship; the conquered nations wanted to be incorporated into the Roman republic. Republican government is not suited well for large areas and diverse peoples. An empire is too large to be ruled by democratic or republican processes. Empire building creates great wealth that has a corrupting effect on the upper classes and destroys the very virtues that enabled the nation to build an empire in the first place. *Which is better: empire or a republic?* The Roman empire brought prosperity, peace and Graeco-Roman culture to the peoples she conquered. For the Roman people, however, the empire brought the loss of self-rule and the impoverishment of the plebeians. The ideal age of Rome is always considered to be the glory days of the Republic, not the decadent empire.

*E. Is the conflict between republican government and empire building applicable to America? Explain.

This question is a good one for many interesting discussions. American military presence, on land and sea, is completely dominant throughout the world and is a *de facto* empire although not an acknowledged one. American commercial and cultural interests are also very dominant in every part of the world. There are many similarities and differences between Rome and America.

Chapter 22
1. Who was one of the greatest orators in the history of Rome? Cicero
2. What mysterious conspiracy to overthrow Rome was defeated by Cicero's eloquent and powerful speeches in the Senate? Catiline conspiracy
3. *These speeches are considered to be the greatest examples of Latin prose, and are often read in high school Latin classes. What are they called? Catiline Orations
4. *When did the events of this chapter occur?
   During the time Caesar was a high priest in Rome, before the Gallic War, 63 B.C.

Chapter 23
1. Name the three men of the Second Triumvirate?
   The Second Triumvirate was Octavius, Antony, Lepidus. (The First Triumvirate was Caesar, Pompey, Crassus)
2. What does triumvirate mean? Rule by three men.
3. Where did the Triumvirate defeat Brutus and how did he die?
   Brutus was defeated at Philippi in Macedonia, and he fell on his sword.
4. In what battle were Antony and Cleopatra defeated by Octavius, and how did they die?
   Octavius defeated Antony and Cleopatra at the battle of Actium. Antony stabbed himself and Cleopatra died from the bite of a poisonous snake called an asp.
5. Who was Julius Caesar's adopted son and nephew? Octavius
6. What was Octavius' name changed to and what does it mean?
   Octavius' name was changed to Augustus, which means sacred.
7. *In what year did the Republic of Rome cease to exist and who is considered to be the first of the long line of Roman emperors? Augustus became emperor in 23 B.C.

History Guide and Key

8. What was the name of the elite military unit that guarded the Roman emperor? Praetorian Guard
9. Name some famous people who lived during the reign of Augustus?
   Horace, Virgil, Varius, Ovid, Livy. Jesus Christ was born during the reign of Caesar Augustus, Luke 2:1.

Chapter 24

1. Name the four emperors of Rome after Augustus who were all tyrants. Tiberius, Caligula, Claudius, Nero
2. How did Nero kill his stepbrother? How did he attempt to kill his mother? Poison, drowning
3. Who did Nero blame for the burning of Rome? Who died during the subsequent persecution?
   Christians. The Apostle Paul was beheaded and Peter was crucified.
4. Name two famous authors who committed suicide upon Nero's orders. Seneca, Lucan
5. *What does the expression "Nero fiddled while Rome burned" mean when applied to current politics?
   It means that the rulers are amusing themselves, instead of attending to the the serious problems of the nation.

Chapter 25

1. Following Nero, three men where made emperors by their soldiers and each ruled for a short time.
   Name them. Galba, Otho, Vitellius
2. Who captured Jerusalem and destroyed the temple of the Jews, fulfilling the prophecy of Christ? In
   what year was the destruction of Jerusalem? Titus destroyed Jerusalem and the temple in 70 A.D
3. *Where in the Bible is Christ's prophecy about the destruction of Jerusalem and what does it say?
   Matthew 24:1-35, especially verses 1,2,34.
4. *What is famous about the Arch of Titus? The Arch of Titus is still standing in the Forum in Rome and its
   carving of the menorah being carried out to the Temple is very clear. It was built to commemorate the destruction of Jerusalem and other accomplishments of Titus.
5. Name three building projects of Titus. Titus finished the Colosseum, and he built the Baths of Titus and the Arch.
6. What two cities were destroyed by the eruption of Mt.Vesuvius during the reign of Titus?
   Pompeii and Herculaneum

Chapter 26

1. Name the two emperors after Titus. Domitian and Nerva
2. Name the three areas that Trajan brought into the Empire. Dacia, Armenia, Mesopotamia
3. Where was the country of Dacia and what is it called today? Hungary, north of the Danube River
4. Where was the country of Armenia and what is it called today? Armenia, between Black Sea and Caspian
   Sea.
5. Where was the area of Mesopotamia and what is it called today? Iraq, between the Tigris and Euphrates R.
6. Name four building projects associated with the reign of Trajan.
   Trajan's Forum, Column, bridge over the Danube, and improved the Circus Maximus
7. After the reign of Trajan, what was the wish of the people of Rome about their future emperors?
   As great as Augustus and as good as Trajan

Chapter 27

1. Name two important building projects of Hadrian that can still be seen today.
   Hadrian's Wall and Hadrian's Tomb
2. What was the purpose of Hadrian's wall and where was it?
   Hadrian's Wall was built in northern Britain to keep the fierce tribes of Scotland from raiding the Roman province of Britain. Photographs of sections of this wall are quite famous.
3. *What became of Hadrian's tomb? It was a huge structure in which many emperors were buried. After the
   fall of Rome it was used as a fortress for the Popes and was connected to the Vatican by an underground passage. It is now called Castle St. Angelo. The bridge over the Tiber River which leads to it is lined with statues
   of angels.
4. Why was Antonius called Pius? He was a good man and kind to Christians.
5. What were the Catacombs?
   The catacombs were underground passages where Christians worshipped and buried their dead.

6. What philosophy did Marcus Aurelius follow? What were the main beliefs of this philosophy? Stoicism. The stoics were followers of Zeno. Stoics believed the highest good was to control one's feelings, experiencing neither joy or sorrow and to do what is right because it is one's duty.
7. What did Marcus Aurelius call his Christian legion and why? The "Thundering Legion," because a sudden rain storm occurred after they had prayed for rain.
8. *In what ways does Marcus Aurelius seem like a Christian? He was very kind, moral, compassionate, not desirous of power or glory. He established good schools and hospitals in Rome.
9. *Why do you think Marcus Aurelius was not happy? What Christian virtues did he not possess? Marcus Aurelius had no hope. He did seem to have love for his fellow man, but he acted out of duty, not out of love for Christ. Marcus Aurelius demonstrates the failure of paganism to offer a religion that fulfills the human heart. He was the best example of a virtuous pagan, yet the dominant note of his life is sadness. Faith, hope and joy. Marcus Aurelius had no faith, therefore he was without hope and thus his life was without joy.

Chapter 28
1. The hundred years after the death of Marcus Aurelius are called by what name? Describe this period. Military anarchy from A.D. 180-285. Increase in taxes, inflation, crime, ruination of middle class.
2. How were the emperors put in power during this period? by the army
3. Who said "The Empire is too big to be ruled by one man" and divided the Empire into two parts? Diocletian
4. Who was the last emperor under which there was widespread persecution of Christians? Diocletian
5. Describe some of the reforms and government reorganizations of Diocletion. He divided the empire into two parts and set up a plan for the peaceful succession of co-emperors. He broke armies and provinces up into smaller units and created an Inspectorate. He established price controls.
6. * Why do you think most of his reforms were unsuccessful? Regulations do not create virtuous citizens. The beliefs and values that created Rome were dying.

Chapter 29
1. Who was the first Roman emperor to become a Christian? Constantine
2. *Constantine saw a vision of a cross before what battle? The battle of Milvian Bridge
3. What words were written on the cross? In hoc signo vinces. In this sign you will conquer.
4. Where did Constantine move the capital of the Roman Empire to, and what did he name the city? He moved the capital to Byzantium which he renamed Constantinople.

Chapter 30
1. What emperor after Constantine tried to reestablish the pagan religion of ancient Rome? Julian the Apostate
2. What did he attempt to do in order to prove the Christian religion untrue? He attempted to rebuild the Temple of Jerusalem, destoyed by Titus, and thereby contradict the prophecy of Christ. The destruction of the Temple was a symbol of God's judgment against the Jews and the replacement of Judaism by Christianity.
3. What happened when work began on the Temple? What did Julian the Apostate say as he was dying? Balls of fire burst from the ground where they were working. "Thou has conquered, O Galilean."
4. Beginning with Valentinian the empire was usually ruled by two emperors. What were they called? Emperor of the East and Emperor of the West.
5. What emperor was publicly shamed by Ambrose, the bishop of Milan? Theodosius had to do penance before returning to church, because he had massacred over 6000 citizens.
6. Who was the last emperor of the West, who replaced him, and in what year did the Roman Empire of the West come to an end? Romulus Augustulus was the last Emperor of the West and he was deposed in A.D. 476 by Odoacer, an Italian soldier from a barbarian tribe who had decided to make himself king.
7. In what year did the Roman Empire of the East come to an end? A.D. 1453

THE IMPERIAL REPUBLIC
264 B.C.- 27 B.C.

264-146 B.C.   **THE PUNIC WARS**

Regulus	1st Punic War, started in Sicily, lost an army in Africa Word of honor and Rome over self
	2nd Punic War, worst defeat in Roman history at Cannae to Hannibal
Fabius	Delaying tactics
Scipio Africanus	Defeated Hannibal at Zama
Cato the Censor	3rd Punic War, Carthage sowed with salt. *Delenda est Carthago*

146-27 B.C.   **THE REPUBLIC BREAKS DOWN**

The Gracchi	Tiberius	Agrarian bill, clubbed to death by senators in Assembly
	Caius	Accused of wanting to be king, died in mob violence
	Marius	Teutones, Cimbri, Ambrones, dictator general, exile in Carthage, vengeance on nobles.

Social War 90-87 B.C.
(war with Italian allies)

	Sulla	Fame in Social War, enemy of Marius. King Mithridates of Pontus Sulla first to bring his army into Rome. Dictator general, massacre of Marians
	Pompey the Great	Pirates, defeated Mithridates, reorganized Asia under Roman rule. Dictator general, 1st Triumvirate - Pompey, Caesar, Crassus

Civil War 49-27 B.C.

	Julius Caesar	Soldier, statesman, scholar, orator Conquest of Gaul - 8 yrs., *De Bello Gallico*, invasion of Britain. Pompey declared Caesar to be an enemy of Rome. Crossed the Rubicon. Dictator of Rome. Julian calendar. Assassinated 44 B.C.
	Cicero	Greatest orator. Catiline orations. Put to death by order of Mark Antony.

THE ROMAN EMPIRE
27 B.C. - 476 A.D.

PAX ROMANA
27 B.C. - 180 A.D.

Augustus
Octavius given title in 27B.C.

Grandnephew of Caesar, adopted son. 2nd Triumvirate - Octavius, Antony, Lepidus. Defeated Brutus and Cassius at Philippi, defeated Antony and Cleopatra at Actium. End of Civil War and beginning of Pax Romana (200 years of peace and prosperity)

Tiberius
Caligula
Claudius
64 A.D. *persecution*   Nero

Jesus crucified during reign of Tiberius
The four tyrant emperors
First Roman persecution of Christians under Nero

Galba
Otho
Vitellius

Generals put in power by army, each for only a few months.

70 A.D.   Vespasian
Titus, his son

Destruction of Jerusalem Arch of Titus, Colosseum, Destruction of Pompeii by Mt. Vesuvius

Domitian   Killed flies

	Nerva	
	Trajan	Enlarged empire: Dacia, Armenia Mesopotamia. Trajan's Forum, Column As great as Augustus and as good as Trajan.
	Hadrian	Hadrian's Wall, Tomb (Castel St. Angelo)
	Antoninus Pius	good to Christians
	Marcus Aurelius	Stoic, Thundering Legion, A virtuous pagan.

MILITARY ANARCHY
180- 285 A.D.

Corruption, taxes, inflation, crime Impoverishment of middle class.

REORGANIZATION AND FALL
OF ROMAN EMPIRE

285. A.D.	Diocletian	Divided empire in two. Emperor of East and Emperor of West. Last widespread persecution of Christians.
307 A.D.	Constantine the Great	The first Christian emperor. Battle of Milvian Bridge. Moved capital from Rome to Constantinople.
363 A.D.	Julian the Apostate	Gave up Christian religion and reconverted to paganism. Tried to rebuild the Temple in Jerusalem.
380 A.D.	Theodosius	Capital of Western empire in Milan. Bishop of Milan, Ambrose, made Theodosius do penance for massacre before he could come to church.

End of Western Empire
476 A.D.	Romulus Augustulus	Last Roman emperor. Deposed by a barbarian soldier, Odoacer

End of Eastern Empire
1453 A.D.		Constantinople fell to the Turks.

Appendices

Selections for memorization give students exposure to real Latin and also provide future texts for translation and illustration of syntax. In addition, these selections expose students to their religious, cultural, and musical heritage. The *Gloria, Sanctus, Gloria Patri*, and *Ave Maria* may be more readily learned by singing in Gregorian chant or listening to music recordings if so desired.

The first two selections are from the Ordinary of the Mass. The Ordinary of the Mass is the part with unchanging text and consists of five parts:

> Kyrie (Lord have mercy)
> Gloria (Glory to God in the highest)
> Credo (The Nicene Creed, beginning, *I believe in one God*)
> Sanctus and Benedictus (Holy, Holy, Holy)
> Agnus Dei ((Lamb of God)

The techniques of harmony and counterpoint, the basis of all European music, came directly from improvising on the singing of the Mass in plainchant. As composers continued to develop musical technique, their primary text was the Ordinary of the Mass in Latin, which became the inspiration for more musical masterpieces than any other source. The great Viennese masters Haydn, Mozart and Schubert wrote some of their most glorious music in their masses. Some of the most famous Masses are Bach's *B-minor Mass*, Beethoven's *Missa Solemnis* and Mozart's *Requiem Mass*. Since the Catholic Church has discarded much of its traditional music, the world has picked it up and now many Protestant and secular music groups perform Gregorian chant, Masses, and other Latin music as part of their cultural and religious heritage.

*The **Gloria** is the Church's great hymn of praise.*

Gloria

Gloria in excelsis Deo	*Glory to God in the highest*
Et in terra pax hominibus bonae voluntatis	*And on earth peace to men of good will.*
Laudamus te, Benedicimus te	*We praise you, we bless you*
Adoramus te, Glorificamus te	*We worship you, we glorify you*
Gratias agimus tibi	*We give you thanks*
Propter magnam gloriam tuam	*because of your great glory*
Domine Deus, Rex caelestis	*Lord God, Heavenly King*
Deus Pater omnipotens.	*Almighty God and Father.*
Domine Fili unigenite Jesu Christe	*Lord Jesus Christ, Only Begotten Son*
Domine Deus, Agnus Dei, Filius Patris	*Lord God, Lamb of God, Son of the Father*
Qui tollis peccata mundi, miserere nobis	*You take away the sins of the world, have mercy on us.*
Qui tollis peccata mundi,	*You take away the sins of the world,*
Suscipe deprecationem nostram.	*Receive our prayer.*
Qui sedes ad dexteram Patris,	*You are seated at the right hand of the Father*
miserere nobis. Quoniam tu solus sanctus.	*Have mercy on us. For you alone are holy*
Tu solus Dominus. Tu solus Altissimus,	*You alone are Lord. You alone are the most high*
Jesu Christe, cum Sancto Spiritu,	*Jesus Christ,with the Holy Spirit*
in gloria Dei Patris. Amen	*in the glory of God the Father. Amen*

Sanctus

Sanctus, Sanctus, Sanctus,	*Holy, holy, holy,*
Dominus Deus Sabaoth	*Lord God of Hosts*
Pleni sunt Caeli et Terra, gloria tua	*Heaven and earth are full of Your glory*
Hosanna in excelsis	*Hosanna in the highest*
Benedictus qui venit in nomine Domini	*Blessed is he who comes in the name of the Lord*
Hosanna in excelsis	*Hosanna in the highest*

A doxology is a hymn of praise to the Trinity. This doxology is also called the **Glory be** *or* **Gloria Patri**, *according to the custom of naming a prayer after its first two words.*

Doxology
(Glory be)

Gloria Patri, et Filio, et Spiritui Sancto	*Glory be to the Father, Son, and Holy Spirit*
Sicut erat in principio et nunc,	*As it was in the beginning, is now*
Et semper et in saecula saeculorum. Amen.	*And ever shall be, world without end. Amen.*

There are many beautiful versions of the Ave Maria. The most famous, by Franz Schubert, scandalized many listeners the first time it was sung in church because of its theatrical style. Schubert's **Ave Maria** *is often called the world's most beautiful song, a fitting tribute to the most honored and revered woman in history, whom William Wordsworth called "our tainted nature's solitary boast."*

Ave Maria

Ave Maria, gratia plena	*Hail Mary, full of grace*
Dominus tecum,	*The Lord is with thee*
Benedicta tu in mulieribus	*Blessed art thou among women*
Et benedictus fructus ventris tui, Jesus	*And blessed is the fruit of thy womb, Jesus*
Sancta Maria, Mater Dei	*Holy Mary, Mother of God*
Ora pro nobis peccatoribus	*Pray for us sinners*
Nunc et in hora mortis nostrae. Amen.	*Now and at the hour of our death. Amen.*

How many of these words do you know or can you figure out? Words learned in this course are underlined.

Genesis 1:1-5

In principio creavit Deus caelum et terram. Terra autem erat inanis et vacua et

tenebrae super faciem abyssi et spiritus Dei ferebatur super aquas. Dixitque [1]

Deus: "Fiat lux." Et facta est lux. Et vidit Deus lucem quod esset bona et divisit

lucem ac tenebras. Appellavitque lucem diem et tenebras noctem. Factumque est

vespere et mane dies unus.

John 1:1-5

In principio erat Verbum et Verbum erat apud Deum et Deus erat Verbum.

Hoc erat in principio apud Deum. Omnia per ipsum facta sunt et sine ipso

factum est nihil. Quod factum est in ipso vita erat et vita erat lux hominum et

lux in tenebris lucet et tenebrae eam non compehenderunt.

[1] **que** added to the end of a word means *and* , also notice **appelavitque** and **factumque** in line 4

| Optime! | *Excellent* |

Pessime! — *Very bad!*

I (ite, pl.) ad januam — *Go to the door*
       fenestram — *window*
       tabulam nigram — *blackboard*

Aperi — *Open*
Claude — *Close*
       januam — *door*
       fenestram — *window*
       librum — *book*

Aperite libros — *Open (your) books*

Me paenitet — *I'm sorry*

Fiat — *All right (let it be done)*

De hoc satis — *Enough of this!*

Collige folia — *Collect the papers*

Ego amo te — *I love you*

Quid dixit — *What did he say?*

Veni Veni Emmanuel

This hymn actually traces its origins to the church liturgy prior to the ninth century. The text is derived from the seven great O antiphons which were said at vespers from Dec 17 to Dec 23. The first English translation appeared in 1851 and it is now a popular Christmas carol, sung in both English and Latin.

Plainsong, 12th Century

Veni Creator Spiritus

This is a vesper hymn for Whitsunday (Pentecost) by Rabanus Maurus, Archbishop of Mainz (d. 856). It is sung at other solemn occasions such as ordinations and dedications of Churches. It is also a traditional hymn for the opening of the school year at academic institutions.

Ve - ni, Cre - - - a - tor Spi - ri - tus,
Qui di - ce - - - ris Pa - - ra - cli - tus,

Men-tes tu - o - rum vi - si - ta: Im - ple su - per - na gra - ti - a
Al - tis - si - mi do - num de - i, Fons vi - vus, ig - nis, ca - ri - tas

Quae tu cre - a - sti pec - to - ra. A - - men.
Et spi - ri - ta - lis unc - ti - o.

Gaudeamus Igitur

Music was an important part of life in medieval Europe, not only in churches, but also in taverns, villages, schools, castles and roadsides. This is the greatest of the medieval student songs, and a jollier, more rousing song would be hard to find. Brahms used its melody in the glorious climax to his "Academic Festival Overture."

GAUDEAMUS IGITUR
Let us rejoice therefore,
while we are young
After delightful youth
After a hard old age
The earth will have us
The earth will have us

Long live the university
Long live the professors
Long live all the graduates
Long live all the undergraduates
May they ever flourish
May they ever flourish

Long live the republic
And those who rule it
Long live our state
Long live this association
Which gathers us to this place
Which gathers us to this place

VENI CREATOR SPIRITUS[1]
Come Creator Spirit
visit the souls of thy people,
fill with grace from on high
the hearts which thou hast created

Thou who art called the Comforter,
gift of the most high God,
living fount, fire, love
and unction of souls.

VENI VENI EMMANUEL
O Come, O come, Emmanuel,
And ransom captive Israel,
That mourns in lonely exile here
Until the son of God appear.
Rejoice, rejoice, Emmanuel
Shall come to thee, O Israel.

O come, thou Rod of Jesse, free
Thine own from Satan's tyranny,
From depths of hell thy people save
And give them victory o're the grave.
Rejoice, rejoice, Emmanuel
Shall come to thee, O Israel.

[1] translation by Adrian Fortescue

Latin Sayings

1. Retro, Satana! — Get thee behind me, Satan!
2. Natura non facit saltum — Nature does not make leaps
3. Magister dixit — The master has spoken
4. Repetitio mater studiorum — Repetition is the mother of learning
5. Hannibal ad portas! — Hannibal at the gates!
6. Errare est humanum *(Seneca)* — To err is human
7. Caveat emptor — Let the buyer beware
8. Credo in unum Deum — I believe in one God
9. Arma virumque cano *(1st line of Aeneid)* — I sing of arms and a man
10. Ave Caesar - morituri te salutamus *(Roman gladiators)* — Hail Caesar - we who are about to die salute you
11. Hodie Christus natus est — Today Christ is born
12. Non oratorem, non senatorem, sed piscatorem. *(St. Augustine)* — Not an orator, not a senator, but a fisherman.
13. Delenda est Carthago *(Cato the elder)* — Carthage must be destroyed
14. Romanus civis sum — I am a citizen of Rome
15. O tempora, O mores *(Cicero)* — O the times, O the customs
16. Etiam capillus unus habet umbram *(Publius Syrus)* — Even one hair has a shadow
17. O, praeclarum custodem ovium lupum. *(Cicero)* — O, excellent protector of sheep, the wolf.
18. Dies Irae — Day of wrath
19. Deo gratias — Thanks be to God

Grammar Forms

VERBS

Regular principal parts

First conjugation	**voco, vocare, vocavi, vocatus**
Second conjugation	**moneo, monére, monui, monitus**
Third conjugation	**rego, regere**
Fourth conjugation	**audio, audire, audivi, auditus**

Present tense

	First conjugation		Second	Third	Fourth	*To be* Verb
S.						
1 P.	**voco**	*I call, am calling, do call*	moneo	rego	audio	sum
2 P.	**vocas**	*you call, are calling, do call*	mones	regis	audis	es
3 P.	**vocat**	*he, she it calls, is calling, does call*	monet	regit	audit	est
Pl.						
1 P.	**vocamus**	*we call, are calling, do call*	monemus	regimus	audimus	sumus
2 P.	**vocatis**	*you call, are calling, do call*	monetis	regitis	auditis	estis
3 P.	**vocant**	*they call, are calling, do call*	monent	regunt	audiunt	sunt

Imperfect tense

			Second	Third	Fourth	
S.						
1 P.	**vocabam**	*I was calling*	monebam	regebam	audiebam	eram
2 P.	**vocabas**	*you were calling*	monebas	regebas	audiebas	eras
3 P.	**vocabat**	*he, she,it was calling*	monebat	regebat	audiebat	erat
Pl.						
1 P.	**vocabamus**	*we were calling*	monebamus	regebamus	audiebamus	eramus
2 P.	**vocabatis**	*you were calling*	monebatis	regebatis	audiebatis	eratis
3 P.	**vocabant**	*they were calling*	monebant	regebant	audiebant	erant

Future tense

			Second	Third	Fourth	
S.						
1 P.	**vocabo**	*I will call*	monebo	-	-	ero
2 P.	**vocabis**	*you will call*	monebis			eris
3 P.	**vocabit**	*he, she, it will call*	monebit			erit
Pl.						
1 P.	**vocabimus**	*we will call*	monebimus	-	-	erimus
2 P.	**vocabitis**	*you will call*	monebitis			eritis
3 P.	**vocabunt**	*they will call*	monebunt			erunt

PRONOUNS

First Person					Second Person			
S.		*Pl.*			*S.*		*Pl.*	
ego	*I*	nos	*we*		tu	*you*	vos	*you*
mei	*me*	nostri,um	*us*		tui	*you*	vestri, um	*you*
mihi	*me*	nobis	*us*		tibi	*you*	vobis	*you*
me	*me*	nos	*us*		te	*you*	vos	*you*
me	*me*	nobis	*us*		te	*you*	vobis	*you*

NOUNS

1st decl. F.   2nd decl. M.   2nd decl. N.

	S.	Pl.	S.	Pl.	S.	Pl.
Nominative	mensa	mensae	servus	servi	donum	dona
Genitive	mensae	mensarum	servi	servorum	doni	donorum
Dative	mensae	mensis	servo	servis	dono	donis
Accusative	mensam	mensas	servum	servos	donum	dona
Ablative	mensa	mensis	servo	servis	dono	donis

3rd decl. M/F   3rd decl. N   i stem   4th decl.   5th decl.

lex	leges	flumen	flumina	pars	partes	portus	portus	res	res
legis	legum	fluminis	fluminum	partis	partium	portus	portuum	rei	rerum
legi	legibus	flumini	fluminibus	parti	partibus	portui	portibus	rei	rebus
legem	leges	flumen	flumina	partem	partes	portum	portus	rem	res
lege	legibus	flumine	fluminibus	parte	partibus	portu	portibus	re	rebus

CASE ENDINGS

1 st decl. F.   2nd decl. M.   2nd decl. N.

S.	Pl.	S.	Pl.	S.	Pl.
a	ae	us,er,ir	i	um	a
ae	arum	i	orum	i	orum
ae	is	o	is	o	is
am	as	um	os	um	a
a	is	o	is	o	is

3rd decl. M/ F.   3rd decl. N   4th decl.   5th decl.

S.	Pl.	S.	Pl.	S.	Pl.	S.	Pl.
—	es	—	a	us	us	es	es
is	ium	is	um	us	uum	ei	erum
i	ibus	i	ibus	ui	ibus	ei	ebus
em	es	—	a	um	us	em	es
e	ibus	e	ibus	u	ibus	e	ebus

ADJECTIVES
First and second declension adjectives

	Masculine		Feminine		Neuter	
	S.	Pl.	S.	Pl.	S.	Pl.
Nominative	bonus	boni	bona	bonae	bonum	bona
Genitive	boni	bonorum	bonae	bonarum	boni	bonorum
Dative	bono	bonis	bonae	bonis	bono	bonis
Accusative	bonum	bonos	bonam	bonas	bonum	bona
Ablative	bono	bonis	bona	bonis	bono	bonis

Vocabulary Index

Latin-English Vocabulary

LATIN	ENGLISH	DERIVATIVE(S)
A		
ab, a, prep. w. abl.	from, away from	
acies, aciei, F	battle line	
ad, (prep. w. acc.)	to, toward, near	
adoro, (1)	adore	adoration
adventus, us, M	arrival, coming	advent, adventure
aeternus, a, um	eternal, everlasting	eternity
ager, agri, M	field (agricultural)	agriculture
agnus, i, M	lamb	
ago, agere	do, drive, act, treat	agent, agile
agricola, ae, M	farmer	agriculture
albus, a, um	white	albino
alienus, a, um	foreign, unfavorable	alien, alienate
almus, a, um	nurturing, kindly	
altus, a, um	high, deep	altitude, altar
ambulo, (1)	walk	ambulance
amicus, i, M	friend	amicable
amo, (1)	love	amorous, amateur
angelus, i, M	angel	angelic
animus, i, M	mind, spirit	animated, animal
annus, i, M	year	annual, annals, anniversary
ante, (prep. w. acc.)	before	antique
aperio, aperire	open	aperture
apostolus, i, M	apostle	
appello, (1)	speak to, address	appeal, appellation
aqua, ae, F	water	aquarium, aqueduct
aquarius	water carrier	
aquila, ae, F	eagle	aquiline
ara, ae, F	altar	
arbor, arboris, F	tree	arboretum, arbor
aries	ram	
aro, (1)	plow	arable
ars, artis, F	art, skill	artist, artificial
audio, (4)	hear	audition,auditorium, audible, audience
augeo, augére	increase	augment
auriga, ae, C	charioteer	
aurora, ae, F	dawn	aurora borealis
autem	however	
auxilium, i, N	help, aid	auxiliary
avis, avis, F	bird	aviation, aviator, aviary
B		
barbarus, i, N	barbarian	barbaric
beatus, a, um	blessed	beatitude
bellum, i, N	war	bellicose, belligerent, rebel
bene	well	benefit, benevolent
bibo, bibere	drink	bib, beverage, imbibe
bonus, a, um	good	bonbon, bonny

LATIN	ENGLISH	DERIVATIVE(S)
C		
cado, cadere	fall	cadence, cascade
caelum, i, N	heaven	celestial
Caesar, Caesaris, M	Caesar	tsar, czar
campus, i, M	field (athletic, assembly)	camp
cancer	crab	
canis, canis, C	dog	canine
cano, canere	sing	canticle, cantata
capillus, i, M	hair	capillary
capricorn	goat	
caput, capitis, N	head	Capitol, capital, capitalize
caritas, caritatis, F	love, charity	care, charity
carmen, carminis, N	song	
casa, ae, F	cottage	casino
caveo, cavére	guard against, beware of	caution
cena, ae, F	dinner	
centum	hundred	cent, century, percent, centennial, centigrade
centurio, centurionis, M	centurion	
certus, a, um	certain, sure	certainly
Christianus, a, um	Christian	
Christianus, i	a Christian	
Christus, i, M	Christ	
cibus, i, M	food	ciborium
circum, (prep. w. acc.)	around, about	
cithara, ae, F	harp	guitar
civis, civis, C	citizen	civil, civilian, civilian
civitas, civitatis, F	state	civil, civility, city, citizen, civilization
clam, adv.	secretly	clandestine
clamo, (1)	shout	clamor, clamorous, exclamation, claim
clamor, clamoris, M	shout, shouting	clamor, clamorous, exclamation
clarus, a, um	clear, bright, famous	clarity, clearance, clarify, clarinet
claudo, claudere	shut	clause, close, closet, claustrophobia
collis, collis, M	hill	
contra (prep. w. acc.)	against	contradict, contrary, contrast
cor, cordis, N	heart	cordial, core, courage
corona, ae, F	crown	coronation
corpus, corporis, N	body	corporal, corpse, corps, corporation
cras, adv.	tomorrow	
credo, credere	believe	credible, incredible, creed, credit
crux, crucis, F	cross	crucifix, crucifixion, crucial
culina, ae, F	kitchen	culinary, kiln
culpa, ae, F	fault, crime	culprit, culpable
cum, prep. w. abl.	with	
cupidus, a, um	eager, desirous	Cupid, cupidity
cur	why	
curro, currere	run	current, currency, concurrent
custos, custodis, M	guard	custody, custodian

Latin-English Vocabulary

LATIN	ENGLISH	DERIVATIVE(S)
D		
de, (prep. w. abl.)	down from	
debeo, (2)	owe, ought	debt, debtor, duty
debitum, i, N	debt, trespass	debit
decem	ten	December
defendo, defendere	defend	defensive, defense, defendant
dens, dentis, M	tooth	dental, dentist
Deus, i, M	God	deity
dico, dicere	say, tell	dictionary, dictator, predict, verdict, contradict
dies, diei, M	day	dial, diary
discipulus, i, M	student	disciple
diu, (adv.)	for a long time	
do, dare, dedi, datus	give	donate, donation, donor
doceo, docére	teach	docile, document, doctrine, indoctrinate
dolor, doloris, M	pain, sorrow	dolorous, Via Dolorosa
dominus, i, M	lord, master	dominate, dominion
donum, i, N	gift	donate, donation, donor
dormio, (4)	sleep	dormitory, dormant, dormer
duco, ducere, duxi, ductus	lead, guide	duke, duchess, abduct, aqueduct, conduct
duo	two	duet, dual, duo, duel
dux, ducis, M	leader	duke, duke, aqueduct
E		
ecclesia, ae, F	church	Ecclesiastes, ecclesiastical
edo, edere	eat	edible
ego, mei	I, me	
epistula, ae, F	letter	epistle
equitatus, us, M	cavalry	equestrian
equus, i, M	horse	equine, equestrian
eram (imperfect of sum)	I was	
ero (future of sum)	I will be	
erro, (1)	err	errant, erratic, aberration
et	and	etcetera
etiam	also, even	
Evangelium, i, N	gospel	evangelist, evangelical, evangelism
ex, (prep. w. abl.)	out of	exit, extra
exercitus, us, M	army	exercise
exspecto, (1)	wait for	expectation
F		
fabula, ae, F	story	fable, fabulous
facies, faciei, F	face	facial, façade
fama, ae, F	fame, rumor, report	famous, infamous
femina, ae, F	woman	feminine, female
fenestra, ae, F	window	
fides, fidei, F	faith, loyalty	fidelity, infidel
filia, ae, F	daughter	filial
filius, i, M	son	filial
finio (4)	finish	final, finite

LATIN	ENGLISH	DERIVATIVE(S)
finis, finis, M	end, boundary	finish, definite
fleo, flére	cry, weep	feeble
flumen, fluminis, N	river	fluid
fons, fontis, N	fountain, spring, source	font, fount
fortuna, ae, F	fortune, chance	fortune, fortunate
forum, i, N	forum	
frater, fratris, M	brother	fraternal, fraternity
fructus, us, M	fruit, profit, enjoyment	fruit
frumentum, i, N	grain, crops	
fuga, ae, F	flight	fugitive, refugee, fugue

G

Gallia, ae, F	Gaul	Gallic
Gallus, i, M	a Gaul	
gaudium, i, N	joy	gaudy
geminus, i, M	twin	
gens, gentis, F	tribe	genitive, progeny, generate, gender
gladius, i, M	sword	gladiator, gladiola
gloria, ae, F	glory, fame	glorious, glorify
gratia, ae, F	grace, thanks	gracious, gratitude

H

habeo, (2)	have	habit
habito, (1)	live, inhabit, dwell	inhabit, habitation
herba, ae, F	herb, plant	herb, herbal, herbivore
heri, adv.	yesterday	
Hispania, ae, F	Spain	Hispanic
hodie	today	
homo, hominis, M	man	homicide, homo sapiens
hora, ae, F	hour	horoscope
hortus, i, M	garden	horticulture
hostis, hostis, C	enemy	host, hostile, hostility

I

ignis, ignis, F	fire	ignite, ignition, igneous
impedio, (4)	hinder	impediment
imperator, imperatoris, M	general, commander	imperative
imperium, i, N	command, empire	imperial, emperor, empire, imperious
impetus, us, M	attack	impetuous
in, (prep. w. acc. or abl.)	in, on, into, against	
injuria, ae, F	injury	injurious
insula, ae, F	island	insulate, insular
inter, (prep. w. acc.)	between, among	interior, intermission, intergalactic, interlude
ira, ae, F	anger	ire, irate
Italia, ae, F	Italy	italics
itaque	therefore	
iter, itineris, N	journey, march, route	itinerary

Latin-English Vocabulary

LATIN	ENGLISH	DERIVATIVE(S)
J		
janua, ae, F	door	Janus, janitor, January
Jesus, Jesu	Jesus	
jubeo, jubére	order, command	
judico, (1)	judge	judiciary, justice
jus, juris, N	right	jury, just, injure
L		
laboro	work	laborious, laboratory
lacus, us, M	lake	
laetus, a, um	happy, glad, joyful	
laudo, (1)	praise	laud, laudable
lavo, (1)	wash	lavatory, lave
lectio, lectionis, F	lesson	lecture
legatus, i, M	lieutenant, envoy	delegate
legio, legionis, F	legion	legionary
leo, leonis	lion	leonine
lex, legis, F	law	legal, legislature
liber, libri, M	book	library
libero, (1)	set free	liberate, liberal, liberty
libertas, libertatis, F	freedom, liberty	
libra	pair of scales	
lingua, ae, F	language, tongue	language, bilingual, linguistic
locus, i. M	place	local, location
longus, a um	long	longitude
Lucia, ae, F	Lucy	
ludus, -i	game, sport, school	ludicrous
luna, ae, F	moon	lunar, lunacy, lunatic
lupus, i, M	wolf	
lux, lucis, F	light	lucid, Lucifer
M		
magister, magistri, M	teacher, master	magistrate, magisterium, majesty
magnus, a, um	large, great	magnify, magnificent
malus, a, um	bad	malady, maladjusted, malice, dismal
mandatum, i, N	commandment	mandate, mandatory
maneo, manére	remain, stay	mansion
Marcus, i	Mark	
mare, maris, N	sea	marine, maritime, submarine
Maria, ae, F	Mary	Mary
mater, matris, F	mother	maternal, matrimony
memoria, ae, F	memory	memorial, memorize
mens, mentis, F	mind	mental
mensa, ae, F	table	mesa
meridies, ei, M	midday, noon	meridian
meus, a, um	my	
miles, militis, M	soldier	military, militia
mille	thousand	mile, million, milligram, millenium
mitto, mittere, misi, missus	send	mission, missionary, emit, omit, admit, transmit, submit,

LATIN	ENGLISH	DERIVATIVE(S)
permit		
moneo (2)	warn	monitor, admonish
mons, montis, M	mountain	mount
mora, ae, F	delay	moratorium
mors, mortis, F	death	mortal, mortality, immortal
mos, moris M	custom	moral
moveo, movére	move	movie, remove, move, movable
multus, a, um	much, many	multiply, multitude
mundus, i, M	world	mundane
munio, (4)	fortify, construct	ammunition, munitions
murus, i, M	wall	mural
N		
narro, (1)	tell	narrator
nato, (1)	swim	natatorium (indoor swimming pool)
natura, ae, F	nature	natural
nauta, ae, M	sailor	nautilus, nautical
navigo, (1)	sail	navigate, navigation
navis, navis, F	ship	navy, naval
nihil	nothing	
nimbus, i, M	cloud	
nix, nivis, F	snow	
nomen, nominis, N	name	nominate, noun, nominative
non	not	nonsense
nos, nostri, (pers. pronoun)	we, us	
novus, a, um	new	novel, novice, innovate, renovate
nox, noctis, F	night	nocturnal, equinox
numquam, adv.	never	
nunc	now	
nuntius, i, M	message, messenger	announce, pronounce
O		
occupo, (1)	seize	occupy, occupation
octo	eight	October
oculus, i, M	eye	ocular, binocular
oppidum, i, N	town	
opus, operis, N	work, deed	operator, operation
orator, oratoris, M	speaker, orator	orator, oratorio, oratory
orbis, orbis, M	world, orbit, circle	orbit
ordo, ordinis, M	order, rank	order, ordain
oro, (1)	pray, speak	oratory, orator
os, oris, N	mouth	oral, orifice
ovis, ovis, F	sheep	
P		
panis, panis, M	bread	pantry, companion
paro, (1)	prepare	preparation
pars, partis, F	part	particle, particular, partial
parvus, a, um	small	

Latin-English Vocabulary

LATIN	ENGLISH	DERIVATIVE(S)
passio, passionis, F	suffering	passion
pastor, pastoris, M	shepherd	pastoral
pater, patris, M	father	paternal, patrician
patria, ae, F	fatherland, country	patriot, patriotic
pax, pacis, F	peace	pacify, pacific, pacifier
peccatum, i, N	sin, mistake	impeccable, peccadillo
pecunia, ae, F	money	pecuniary, peculiar (from pecus, cow)
per, prep. w. acc.	through	
periculum, i, N	danger, peril	peril, perilous
pes, pedis, M	foot	pedal, centipede, pedestrian, impede, impediment
peto, petere	seek, beg	petition
piscator, piscatoris, M	fisherman	
pisces	fish	
placeo, placére	please	pleasant, placid
plenus, a, um	full	plenary, plenty, plentiful
poeta, ae, M	poet	poetry
pono, ponere, posui, positus	put, place, set	exponent, position, postpone
pons, pontis, M	bridge	pontoon
populus, i, M	people	population, popular
porta, ae, F	gate, door	porch, portal, porthole
porto, (1)	carry	portable, transport, export, import
portus, us, M	harbor	port, seaport
post, prep. w. acc.	after, behind	posterior, posterity
praemium, i, N	reward	premium
primus, a, um	first	primary, prime
principium, i, N	beginning, foundation	principle, principle
proelium, i, N	battle	
prohibeo, (2)	prevent	prohibit
provincia, ae, F	province	
proximus, a, um	next, nearest	proximity, approximate
puella, ae, F	girl	
puer, pueri, M	boy	puerile
pugna, ae, F	fight	pugnacious, repugnant
pugno, (1)	fight	pugnacious
punio, (4)	punish	punitive
Q		
quattuor	four	quart, quarter, quartet (from quartus, fourth)
quid	what	
quinque	five	quintuplets (from quintus, fifth)
quis	who	
quod	because	
R		
regina, ae, F	queen	
regnum, i, N	kingdom	
rego, regere	rule	regal, direct
res, rei, F	thing	real, republic
respondeo, respondére	respond, answer	respond, respond

Latin-English Vocabulary

LATIN	ENGLISH	DERIVATIVE(S)
rex, regis, M	king	regal, Tyrannosaurus Rex
rideo, ridére	laugh	ridicule, ridiculous
Roma, ae, F	Rome	Roman
Romanus, a, um	Roman	
Romanus, i, M	a Roman	
rus, ruris, N	countryside	rural
S		
saeculum, i, N	time, period, age, world	secular
saepe	often	
sagittarius	archer	
sal, salis, M	salt, sea water	saline
saluto, (1)	greet	salutation, salute
sanctus, a, um	holy, saint	sanctify, sanctification, sanctuary
scientia, ae, F	knowledge	science, conscience, conscious, omniscient
scio, (4)	know	science, conscience, conscious
scorpio	scorpion	
scribo, scribere	write	scribe, describe, postscript, scripture, scribble
scutum, i, N	shield	escutcheon (coat of arms shield)
secundus, a, um	second	secondary, second
sed	but	
sedeo, sedére	sit	sedentary, sediment, sedate
sedes, sedis, F	seat, abode	sedentary, sedimentary
sella, ae, F	chair	
semper	always	
senator, senatoris, M	senator	
senatus, us, M	senate	
sentio, sentire	feel, perceive, think	sensitive, resent, sentimental, sentiment
septem	seven	September
servo, (1)	guard, keep	conserve, conservative
servus, i, M	slave, servant	service, servant, servile
sex	six	sextet
sicut	as	
signum, i, N	sign, standard	signal, signature, insignia, design
silva, ae, F	forest	sylvan, Pennsylvania, Transylvania
sine, prep. w. abl.	without	
socius, i, M	ally	social, society
sol, solis, M	sun	solar, solstice, parasol
solus, a, um	alone, only	solitary, solitude, solo
soror, sororis, F	sister	sorority
specto, (1)	look at	spectacle, inspect, spectator, spectacular
spes, spei, F	hope	despair, desperado
spiritus, us, M	spirit	spiritual
statim	immediately	
stella , ae, F	star	stellar
sto, stare, steti, status	stand	stable, station, status
studium, i, N	enthusiasm, zeal, learning	study, student, studious, studio
sub, (prep. w. acc. or abl.)	under, at foot of	submarine, subway
sum	I am	

Latin-English Vocabulary

LATIN	ENGLISH	DERIVATIVE(S)
summus, a, um	highest	summit, sum
supero, (1)	overcome, conquer	superior
supra, (prep. w/ acc.)	over, above	supranational

T

LATIN	ENGLISH	DERIVATIVE(S)
tabella, ae, F	tablet	
taberna, ae, F	shop	tavern, tabernacle
taurus, i, M	bull	
telum, i, N	weapon, dart	
tempto, (1)	tempt	temptation
tempus, temporis, N	time	temporal, tempo, tense
teneo, tenére	hold	tenant, tenacious
tentatio, tentationis, F	temptation	temptation
tergum, i, N	back	
terra, ae, F	land, earth	terrestrial, terrain, territory, Mediterranean
terreo, (2)	frighten, terrify	terrify
tertius, a, um	third	tertiary
timeo, timére	fear	timid, intimidate
timor, timoris, M	fear	timorous, timid, intimidate
toga, ae, F	toga	toga
tollo, tollere	take away, raise up	tolerance
totus, a, um	whole	total
trado, tradere	hand over, deliver up	tradition
trans, (prep. w. acc.)	across	
tres	three	trio, triangle
tu, tui, (pers. pronoun, sing.)	you	
tuba, ae, F	trumpet	tube
tum	then, at that time	
tutus, a, um	safe	
tuus, a, um	your (one person)	

U

LATIN	ENGLISH	DERIVATIVE(S)
ubi	where	
umbra, ae, F	shadow	umbrella
unda, ae, F	wave	undulate, inundate
unus	one	unity, universe, union, unit, unique
undique	from all sides	
urbs, urbis, F	city	urban, suburb
ursa, ae, F	bear	Ursa Major, Ursa Minor
usus, us, M	use, experience	

V

LATIN	ENGLISH	DERIVATIVE(S)
valeo, valére	am well, am strong	valiant, valuable
vallum, i, N	wall, rampart	
venio, venire	come	advent, intervene, event
ventus, i, M	wind	vent, ventilate
ver, veris, N	spring	vernal
verbum, i, N	word	verbal, verbose, verb
veritas, veritatis , F	truth	verity, verify, very

LATIN	ENGLISH	DERIVATIVE(S)
verus, a, um	true	verily, verify, verdict
via, ae, F	road, way	viaduct, via
victoria, ae, F	victory	victorious
vicus, i, M	town, village	vicinity
video, vidére	see	evident, vision, video
villa, ae, F	farmhouse	village, villain
vinco, vincere, vici, victus	conquer	convict, invincible
vinum, i, N	wine	vine, vineyard
vir, viri, M	man	virtue, virile, virtual, triumvirate
virgo, virginis, F	virgin	
virtus, virtutis, F	virtue, courage	virtuous, virtue
vita, ae, F	life	vital, vitamin
vivo, vivere	live	revive, vivid, revival
voco, (1)	call	vocation, vocal, vocabulary
voluntas, voluntatis, F	will, good will	voluntary
vos, vestri, (pers. pronoun, pl.)	you	
vox, vocis, F	voice	vocal, vocation
vulnus, vulneris, N	wound	vulnerable, invulnerable

Key to Abbreviations

F	-	feminine gender
M	-	masculine gender
C	-	common gender

pers.	personal
sing.	singular
pl.	plural
prep.	preposition
adv.	adverb
acc.	accusative
abl.	ablative

Difficult conjugations or delcensions are denoted by (#) after the Latin word

English-Latin Vocabulary

across	trans, prep. w. acc.	drink	bibo, bibere
adore	adoro, (1)	eager, desirous	cupidus, a, um
after, behind	post, prep. w. acc.	eagle	aquila, ae, F
against	contra, prep. w. acc.	eat	edo, edere
ally	socius, i, M	eight	octo
alone, only	solus, a, um	end, boundary	finis, finis, M
also, even	etiam	enemy	hostis, hostis, C
altar	ara, ae, F	enthusiasm, zeal, learning	studium, i, N
always	semper	err	erro, (1)
am well, am strong	valeo, valére	eternal, everlasting	aeternus, a, um
and	et	eye	oculus, i, M
angel	angelus, i, M	face	facies, faciei, F
anger	ira, ae, F	faith, loyalty	fides, fidei, F
apostle	apostolus, i, M	fall	cado, cadere
archer	sagittarius	fame, rumor, report	fama, ae, F
army	exercitus, us, M	farmer	agricola, ae, M
around, about	circum, (prep. w. acc.)	farmhouse	villa, ae, F
arrival, coming	adventus, us, M	father	pater, patris, M
art, skill	ars, artis, F	fatherland, country	patria, ae, F
as	sicut	fault, crime	culpa, ae, F
attack	impetus, us, M	fear	timeo, timére
back	tergum, i, N	fear	timor, timoris, M
bad	malus, a, um	feel, perceive, think	sentio, sentire
barbarian	barbarus, i, N	field (agricultural)	ager, agri, M
battle	proelium, i, N	field (athletic, assembly)	campus, i, M
battle line	acies, aciei, F	fight	pugna, ae, F
bear	ursa, ae, F	fight	pugno, (1)
because	quod	finish	finio (4)
before	ante, prep. w. acc.	fire	ignis, ignis, F
beginning, foundation	principium, i, N	first	primus, a, um
believe	credo, credere	fish	pisces
between, among	inter, prep. w. acc.	fisherman	piscator, piscatoris, M
bird	avis, avis, F	five	quinque
blessed	beatus, a, um	flight	fuga, ae, F
body	corpus, corporis, N	food	cibus, i, M
book	liber, libri, M	foot	pes, pedis, M
boy	puer, pueri, M	for a long time	diu, adv.
bread	panis, panis, M	foreign, unfavorable	alienus, a, um
bridge	pons, pontis, M	forest	silva, ae, F
brother	frater, fratris, M	fortify, construct	munio, (4)
bull	taurus, i, M	fortune, chance	fortuna, ae, F
but	sed	forum	forum, i, N
Caesar	Caesar, Caesaris, M	fountain, spring, source	fons, fontis, N
call	voco, (1)	four	quattuor
carry	porto, (1)	freedom, liberty	libertas, libertatis, F
cavalry	equitatus, us, M	friend	amicus, i, M
centurion	centurio, centurionis, M	frighten, terrify	terreo, (2)
certain, sure	certus, a, um	from all sides	undique
chair	sella, ae, F	from, away from	ab, a, prep. w. abl.
charioteer	auriga, ae, C	fruit, profit, enjoyment	fructus, us, M
Christ	Christus, i, M	full	plenus, a, um
Christian	Christianus, a, um	game, sport, school	ludus, -i
Christian, a	Christianus, i	garden	hortus, i, M
church	ecclesia, ae, F	gate, door	porta, ae, F
citizen	civis, civis, C	Gaul	Gallia, ae, F
city	urbs, urbis, F	Gaul, a	Gallus, i, M
clear, bright, famous	clarus, a, um	general, commander	imperator, imperatoris, M
cloud	nimbus, i, M	gift	donum, i, N
come	venio, venire	girl	puella, ae, F
command, empire	imperium, i, N	give	do, dare, dedi, datus
commandment	mandatum, i, N	glory, fame	gloria, ae, F
conquer	vinco, vincere, vici, victus	goat	capricorn
cottage	casa, ae, F	God	Deus, i, M
countryside	rus, ruris, N	good	bonus, a, um
crab	cancer	gospel	Evangelium, i, N
cross	crux, crucis, F	grace, thanks	gratia, ae, F
crown	corona, ae, F	grain, crops	frumentum, i, N
cry, weep	fleo, flére	greet	saluto, (1)
custom	mos, moris M	guard	custos, custodis, M
danger, peril	periculum, i, N	guard against, beware of	caveo, cavére
daughter	filia, ae, F	guard, keep	servo, (1)
dawn	aurora, ae, F	hair	capillus, i, M
day	dies, diei, M	hand over, deliver up	trado, tradere
death	mors, mortis, F	happy, glad, joyful	laetus, a, um
debt, trespass	debitum, i, N	harbor	portus, us, M
defend	defendo, defendere	harp	cithara, ae, F
delay	mora, ae, F	have	habeo, (2)
dinner	cena, ae, F	head	caput, capitis, N
do, drive, act, treat	ago, agere	hear	audio, (4)
dog	canis, canis, C	heart	cor, cordis, N
door	janua, ae, F	heaven	caelum, i, N
down from	de, prep. w. abl.	help, aid	auxilium, i, N

English-Latin Vocabulary

herb, plant	herba, ae, F	often	saepe
high, deep	altus, a, um	one	unus
highest	summus, a, um	open	aperio, aperire
hill	collis, collis, M	order, command	jubeo, jubére
hinder	impedio, (4)	order, rank	ordo, ordinis, M
hold	teneo, tenére	out of	ex, prep. w. abl.
holy, saint	sanctus, a, um	over, above	supra, prep. w. acc.
hope	spes, spei, F	overcome, conquer	supero, (1)
horse	equus, i, M	owe, ought	debeo, (2)
hour	hora, ae, F	pain, sorrow	dolor, doloris, M
however	autem	pair of scales	libra
hundred	centum	part	pars, partis, F
I am	sum	peace	pax, pacis, F
I was	eram (Imperfect of sum)	people	populus, i, M
I will be	ero (Future of sum)	place	locus, i. M
I, me	ego, mei	please	placeo, placére
immediately	statim	plow	aro, (1)
in, on, into, against	in, prep. w. acc. or abl.	poet	poeta, ae, M
increase	augeo, augére	praise	laudo, (1)
injury	injuria, ae, F	pray, speak	oro, (1)
island	insula, ae, F	prepare	paro, (1)
Italy	Italia, ae, F	prevent	prohibeo, (2)
Jesus	Jesus, Jesu	province	provincia, ae, F
journey, march, route	iter, itineris, N	punish	punio, (4)
joy	gaudium, i, N	put, place, set	pono, ponere, posui, positus
judge	judico, (1)	queen	regina, ae, F
king	rex, regis, M	ram	aries
kingdom	regnum, i, N	remain, stay	maneo, manére
kitchen	culina, ae, F	respond, answer	respondeo, respondére
know	scio, (4)	reward	praemium, i, N
knowledge	scientia, ae, F	right	jus, juris, N
lake	lacus, us, M	river	flumen, fluminis, N
lamb	agnus, i, M	road, way	via, ae, F
land, earth	terra, ae, F	Roman	Romanus, a, um
language, tongue	lingua, ae, F	Roman, a	Romanus, i, M
large, great	magnus, a, um	Rome	Roma, ae, F
laugh	rideo, ridére	rule	rego, regere
law	lex, legis, F	run	curro, currere
lead, guide	duco, ducere, duxi, ductus	safe	tutus, a, um
leader	dux, ducis, M	sail	navigo, (1)
legion	legio, legionis, F	sailor	nauta, ae, M
lesson	lectio, lectionis, F	salt, sea water	sal, salis, M
letter	epistula, ae, F	say, tell	dico, dicere
lieutenant, envoy	legatus, i, M	scorpion	scorpio
life	vita, ae, F	sea	mare, maris, N
light	lux, lucis, F	seat, abode	sedes, sedis, F
lion	leo, leonis	second	secundus, a, um
live	vivo, vivere	secretly	clam, adv.
live, inhabit, dwell	habito, (1)	see	video, vidére
long	longus, a um	seek, beg	peto, petere
look at	specto, (1)	seize	occupo, (1)
lord, master	dominus, i, M	senate	senatus, us, M
love	amo, (1)	senator	senator, senatoris, M
love, charity	caritas, caritatis, F	send	mitto, mittere, misi, missus
Lucy	Lucia, ae, F	set free	libero, (1)
man	homo, hominis, M	seven	septem
man	vir, viri, M	shadow	umbra, ae, F
Mark	Marcus, i	sheep	ovis, ovis, F
Mary	Maria, ae, F	shepherd	pastor, pastoris, M
memory	memoria, ae, F	shield	scutum, i, N
message, messenger	nuntius, i, M	ship	navis, navis, F
midday, noon	meridies, ei, M	shop	taberna, ae, F
mind	mens, mentis, F	shout	clamo, (1)
mind, spirit	animus, i, M	shout, shouting	clamor, clamoris, M
money	pecunia, ae, F	shut	claudo, claudere
moon	luna, ae, F	sign, standard	signum, i, N
mother	mater, matris, F	sin, mistake	peccatum, i, N
mountain	mons, montis, M	sing	cano, canere
mouth	os, oris, N	sister	soror, sororis, F
move	moveo, movére	sit	sedeo, sedére
much, many	multus, a, um	six	sex
my	meus, a, um	slave, servant	servus, i, M
name	nomen, nominis, N	sleep	dormio, (4)
nature	natura, ae, F	small	parvus, a, um
never	numquam, adv.	snow	nix, nivis, F
new	novus, a, um	soldier	miles, militis, M
next, nearest	proximus, a, um	son	filius, i, M
night	nox, noctis, F	song	carmen, carminis, N
not	non	Spain	Hispania, ae, F
nothing	nihil	speak to, address	appello, (1)
now	nunc	speaker, orator	orator, oratoris, M
nurturing, kindly	almus, a, um	spirit	spiritus, us, M

English-Latin Vocabulary

spring	ver, veris, N	victory	victoria, ae, F
stand	sto, stare, steti, status	virgin	virgo, virginis, F
star	stella , ae, F	virtue, courage	virtus, virtutis, F
state	civitas, civitatis, F	voice	vox, vocis, F
story	fabula, ae, F	wait for	exspecto, (1)
student	discipulus, i, M	walk	ambulo, (1)
suffering	passio, passionis, F	wall	murus, i, M
sun	sol, solis, M	wall, rampart	vallum, i, N
swim	nato, (1)	war	bellum, i, N
sword	gladius, i, M	warn	moneo (2)
table	mensa, ae, F	wash	lavo, (1)
tablet	tabella, ae, F	water	aqua, ae, F
take away, raise up	tollo, tollere	water carrier	aquarius
teach	doceo, docére	wave	unda, ae, F
teacher, master	magister, magistri, M	we, us	nos, nostri, (personal pronoun)
tell	narro, (1)	weapon, dart	telum, i, N
tempt	tempto, (1)	well	bene
temptation	tentatio, tentationis, F	what	quid
ten	decem	where	ubi
then, at that time	tum	white	albus, a, um
therefore	itaque	who	quis
thing	res, rei, F	whole	totus, a, um
third	tertius, a, um	why	cur
thousand	mille	will, good will	voluntas, voluntatis, F
three	tres	wind	ventus, i, M
through	per, prep. w. acc.	window	fenestra, ae, F
time	tempus, temporis, N	wine	vinum, i, N
time, period, age, world	saeculum, i, N	with	cum, prep. w. abl.
to, toward, near	ad, prep. w. acc.	without	sine, prep. w. abl.
today	hodie	wolf	lupus, i, M
toga	toga, ae, F	woman	femina, ae, F
tomorrow	cras, adv.	word	verbum, i, N
tooth	dens, dentis, M	work	laboro
town	oppidum, i, N	work, deed	opus, operis, N
town, village	vicus, i, M	world	mundus, i, M
tree	arbor, arboris, F	world, orbit, circle	orbis, orbis, M
tribe	gens, gentis, F	wound	vulnus, vulneris, N
true	verus, a, um	write	scribo, scribere
trumpet	tuba, ae, F	year	annus, i, M
truth	veritas, veritatis , F	yesterday	heri, adv.
twin	geminus, i, M	you	tu, tui, personal pronoun, sing.
two	duo	you	vos, vestri, personal pronoun, plural
under, at foot of	sub, prep. w. acc. or abl.	your (one person)	tuus, a, um
use, experience	usus, us, M		